MADE IN
NEW
ZEALAND

MADE IN NEW ZEALAND

Stories of iconic Kiwi brands

Nicola McCloy

RANDOM HOUSE
NEW ZEALAND

FOR THE INVY GIRLS

For more information about our titles go to www.randomhouse.co.nz

A catalogue record for this book is available from the National Library of New Zealand

A RANDOM HOUSE BOOK
published by
Random House New Zealand
18 Poland Road, Glenfield, Auckland, New Zealand

First published 2008

ISBN 978 1 86979 018 9

Design: Nick Turzynski, redinc., Auckland
Cover illustration: Photo New Zealand/Albany
Front flap: Brian McCloy
Back flap: Nicola McCloy
Printed in China by South China Printing Co Ltd

Contents

Introduction **9**

1 KIWI KAI 10

Tip Top ice cream **12**
Georgie Pie **15**
Moro bars **16**
Highlander condensed milk **18**
Chesdale cheese **20**
Edmonds **23**
Griffin's **26**
Eta **28**
Whittaker's **29**
Eskimo Pies **31**

2 ON THE MAP 34

Yarrows Family Bakers **36**
Temuka pottery **38**
Lemon and Paeroa **39**
Barker's of Geraldine **41**
Glaxo **43**
Norsewear **45**
Wattie's **46**
Jimmy's Pies **49**

3 WEARABLE WONDERS 52

Hallensteins **54**
Jandals **56**
Swanndri **57**
Bendon **60**
Skellerup Red Bands **62**
Canterbury rugby jerseys **64**
Stubbies **66**

4 BREAKFAST TIME 68

Vogel's **70**
Anathoth **71**
Sanitarium **74**
Chelsea Sugar **77**
Bell Tea **79**
Gregg's coffee **81**
Creamoata **83**
Crown Lynn **85**

5 AROUND THE HOUSE 88

Tux dog biscuits **90**
Masport lawnmowers **92**
Yates **94**
Resene Paints **97**
Para Pools **99**
Fisher & Paykel **101**
Tullen Snips **103**
Fairydown **105**

6 LIQUID REFRESHMENT 108

Speight's **110**
Hansells **113**
Tui beer **115**
Mac's **118**
Corbans **119**
Steinlager **122**
Wohnsiedler **124**
Monteith's **126**

7 RETAIL THERAPY 128

Four Square **130**
Smith & Caughey's **132**
Foodtown **135**
Arthur Barnett **138**
Kirkcaldie & Stains **141**
Ballantynes **143**

8 VISITORS FROM OVERSEAS 146

Maggi onion soup **148**
Jaffas **150**
Vegemite **151**
Electrolux vacuum cleaners **153**
Kiwi shoe polish **155**
Milo **157**
La-Z-Boy chairs **159**
Sunlight soap **161**
Cadbury **162**

Bibliography **167**

Image credits **172**

Acknowledgements **173**

Also by Nicola McCloy **174**

Introduction

When I first started thinking about writing this book I decided to ask some friends what iconic Kiwi brands, products or companies they'd be keen to find out more about. Their response was fantastic — and a little surprising.

My sister came up with some things from when we were kids that I'd completely forgotten — like Manda ice cream, Jack's chips and Freshbake bread. The top of my brother's list was, somewhat unsurprisingly, Speight's. Claire in Glasgow got a wee bit homesick when she sent through a lengthy list that included Wattie's tomato sauce, Maggi dip and Peanut Slabs. Cathy in Wellington is married to an Englishman, and still she suggested Stubbies! Rochelle is a Four Square baby born on the anniversary of the founding of the grocery co-op, and she's got the certificate to prove it. Kim in Melbourne's list was topped with Kiwi shoe polish — not surprising for someone with a shoe addiction to rival Imelda Marcos. Mel in Dunedin's list prompted a lengthy discussion about Tiger tea, which led us to discover that you can only buy it in the South Island. And Angela's list — well, she just wanted to get her name in a book . . . With all their sage advice safely on board, the list of companies and products was a very long one.

This book covers just a small sample of things that Kiwis have invented, built, made, manufactured or just loved. It's a testament to our collective inventiveness, innovation, entrepreneurship and ability to make something pretty flash out of not very much. To everyone who has had anything to do with the products in the book — thanks, you've made our country a much more interesting place to live.

— Nic McCloy

1

There are few things that evoke memories as clearly and as quickly as food. Whether it's a favourite chocolate bar from your childhood or a breakfast you had to be forced to eat before you went to school, just one smell or mention can bring those memories flooding back . . .

Tip Top ice cream

New Zealanders love ice cream so much that our biggest ice cream company produces 50 million litres of the stuff a year. OK, so they export a lot of that to Japan, Malaysia, Australia, the Pacific and the Caribbean, but we still eat a fair chunk of the frozen dairy dessert every year. It's not just rugby, cricket and netball where we battle with Australia to lead the world — it's ice cream consumption too. The highest average per capita ice cream consumption in the world seesaws between New Zealand and Australia, with Kiwis averaging about 23 litres of the stuff each every year! Who makes most of the ice cream we eat? Well, that's easy, it's Tip Top.

The Tip Top story started in 1936 when a Dunedin ice cream factory manager, Len Malaghan, and one of his customers, Albert Hayman, decided to open a shop selling ice creams and milk shakes in Wellington's Manners St. It was to be New Zealand's first milk bar.

They wanted the place to have a catchy name that described their product. Legend has it that one evening when Malaghan and Hayman were in the dining car of the Kingston Flyer — the passenger train that linked up with the TSS *Earnslaw* to carry people to and from Queenstown — they overheard another diner describe his dinner as having been 'tip top'.

Hayman and Malaghan knew straight away that was how they wanted people to describe their ice cream, and so the Tip Top brand was born. Before the year was out the pair had opened a second ice cream parlour in Wellington and had even branched out to open one in Dunedin. By 1937 the ice cream was so popular the company opened a factory in Wellington to supply demand.

13
Kiwi kai

Within a couple of years Tip Top ice cream was being devoured throughout the lower North Island, in Nelson, Marlborough, Auckland and Otago. The Second World War saw production slow down, but the ice cream became a hit with visiting American servicemen, who couldn't get enough of it.

After the war, the company branched out from just making ice cream to introduce treats like the Eskimo Pie (see page 31), Jelly Tips, Topsys, TT2s and Toppas. By 1962, Tip Top was so popular that the company decided to expand its production. To do this they bought a huge piece of land south of Auckland city and built a state-of-the-art ice cream factory, along with staff housing and a small farm. The factory site has become so much a part of the Auckland landscape that the section of the southern motorway that it sits next to has become known as Tip Top Corner!

The company has changed ownership a few times in its more than 70-year life but one thing hasn't changed — and that's the fact that New Zealanders don't seem to be able to get enough of Tip Top products. In fact, Tip Top produces a whopping 5.5 million Trumpets a year. Not bad for an ice cream that was first introduced in 1964 — so maybe you really can't beat a Trumpet!

MADE IN NEW ZEALAND

Georgie Pie

Georgie Porgie, puddin' and pie,
Kissed the girls and made them cry,
When the boys came out to play
Georgie Porgie ran away.

This seventeenth-century European nursery rhyme might seem a strange way to start a tale about New Zealand's love of fast food, but in some ways it's a real reflection of the story of our very own homegrown fast-food chain — Georgie Pie. The first link is that the Georgie Pie name is thought to have been derived from the nursery rhyme — that part's obvious.

Pudding and pie, well, they were Georgie Pie's specialities. Sometimes they even combined the two into a fruit pie. For people who don't remember the Georgie Pie chain, it was an attempt by a New Zealand company to take on the fast-food giants, McDonald's, Burger King and KFC, with a typically New Zealand treat — pies.

The brand came into being in 1977 with a single restaurant in Auckland. Gradually the chain expanded, until in the 1990s Georgie Pie restaurants started to pop up all over the country. By 1994 there were 26 restaurants, serving 600,000 pies a week!

The Georgie Pie menu was a simple one. Everything was either one, two, three or four dollars. They offered a variety of meat, vegetable and fruit pie options, but the most popular were always good old mince or mince and cheese (with a little bit of competition from the apple pie). It wasn't all pies though — they also did chips, and the magic combination of ice cream and chocolate that was the Buzz Bar sundae.

I don't know about kissing the girls, but when the announcement came in 1996 that the chain's owners were closing it down and selling it to McDonald's there was plenty of crying going on — a lot of it by bereft students who lived on the $1 pies! Seventeen Georgies were converted into McDonald's franchises, and the other 15 were sold to become, among other things, a pet shop, a blood bank and a hardware store. The location of the last-ever Georgie Pie seems to be under debate — was it the one in South Auckland's Hunters Plaza or was it in Glenfield on Auckland's North Shore? What is certain is that Georgie Pie had run away.

Will he ever come back? Well, he just might if a group on social networking site Facebook get their way! The group, cunningly called Bring Back Georgie Pie, had over 10,600 members at the time of writing, including the lithe Kiwi singing star Hayley Westenra. Conversely their opposing group, Don't Bring Back Georgie Pie, boasts a massive membership of 11 people!

Moro bars

You can get them deepfried in batter, you can have them melted in the microwave and poured over ice cream as sauce, you can have them melted with rice bubbles as a slice — but the best way to have them is straight out of the wrapper. There's nothing like a fresh Dunedin-made Moro au naturel!

Since Moros (pronounced More-o and not Mo-ro — as in tomorrow) were invented in this country, New Zealanders have become completely addicted to them. In fact, the Moro is this country's biggest-selling chocolate bar. If you don't believe me, ask Cadbury's — they reckon there's one Moro eaten every two seconds of every day! They also say that if you stacked a year's worth of Moros end to end they'd be 500 times higher than Mt Cook (not to mention a nuisance to passing air traffic!)

The delicious combination of nougat, caramel and chocolate has certainly taken this country by storm, but for a while in the early days our beloved Moro was almost eclipsed by an imported bar from across the Tasman.

It all started in Dunedin back in the 1960s (which, I guess, could be said about a lot of things!). The economy was loosening up, people had a bit of money to spend and New Zealanders were indulging their sweet tooths — or is that teeth? The problem was that they'd taken to a chocolate bar that was being brought in from Australia — you guessed it, the Mars bar.

Now Mars bars are mega-popular in England and Australia, and the folk at Cadbury in Dunedin decided they needed to head off this new bar on the block. They had a bit of a think and came up with a bar that, while being a little bit similar to Mars, was also quite different — and all our own. They got some sample versions of these new bars made and headed to Southland to see what the locals reckoned. The chocolate bars went down a storm and Cadbury realised they were on to something — although had the new bar turned out to be a flop, its popularity there could have been put down to the fact that Southlanders love free stuff!

They named their new bar Moro ('more' with an 'o' on the end of it) and got it into the shops in 1967. They did heaps of advertising and what do you know? Kiwis loved it. Soon the Moro was outselling the Mars bar by heaps. By the 1980s the Mars was starting to make a bit of a comeback, and Cadbury's soon worked out why — a Mars weighed 60 grams, whereas the Moro was only 48 grams. Straight away they upped the size of the Kiwi bar and made sure everyone knew about it. Then something kind of bad but kind of good happened . . .

A few people wrote to television consumer affairs show *Fair Go* saying they weren't getting more go from their Moros — they weren't actually 20 per cent bigger at all. Cadbury's realised some old stock had been sent out by mistake, and decided to put it right by agreeing to give anyone with undersize Moros three bars as replacements. While it could have been a nightmare for Cadbury's, sales of Moros skyrocketed as a result of the positive press (or possibly there were heaps of people buying them up in the hope of getting the magic undersize bar to trade in!).

The Moro is now sold on a limited basis in Australia (getting back at Mars!) and a bar of the same name and a similar make-up is made and sold in Ireland.

Highlander condensed milk

When I was a kid I could never understand why my mother inflicted homemade egg and oil mayonnaise on us. It just didn't seem fair. We had this weird mayonnaise when everyone else we knew had proper mayonnaise made with condensed milk and vinegar. One of my friends' mums was famous for her dressing, which she kept in a Tupperware container in the fridge — it was delicious.

It seems that Mum might have been a bit ahead of her time serving up aioli in Invercargill in the seventies, but the lure of that condensed milk salad dressing is still strong. Little did I know it at the time, but the key ingredient had first been produced in New Zealand at a factory just out of Invercargill in a wee place called Underwood. The Underwood Milk Condensory was built in 1890, making the most of the milk produced on dairy farms on Southland's fertile plains.

Condensed milk was a relatively new product then, having been invented in the United States by Gail Borden in 1856. The product was developed as a way of storing milk and preventing it going off (bear in mind that people didn't have fridges back then). Before that, ships on long sea voyages would sometimes carry cows to provide milk for the crew and passengers.

Condensed milk was produced by using heat to remove a lot of the water — evaporated milk is made the same way. The condensed milk then has plenty of sugar added and is put in airtight tins. Processed like this the milk can last for a very long time, and it tastes pretty good too!

The Underwood factory started making condensed milk in 1890 and marketed it under the Highlander brand. This was appropriate because Southland was home to plenty of people of Scottish origin — it's how they got their distinctive rolling 'r', their love of porridge and the word 'wee', and the name of their Super 14 team.

With the Highlander name came Highlander branding, including the famous piper who still appears on Highlander tins. The original Highlander drawing is thought to have been based on Drum Major James Macgregor of the Invercargill Pipe Band.

The earliest advertising for Highlander Condensed Milk describes it as excellent for children. Well, that's what I think it says. The ad from the early 1900s actually reads:

Hech! Ma bairnies, sook awa! I can be a mither tae ye till yer ain comes back noo I've gotten the rael Hielander Brand Milk.

In 1901, WT Murray & Co took over the Underwood factory. Determined to make sure the product continued to be successful, they ensured stringent hygiene conditions were met before accepting milk from the farmers. Another way they achieved strong sales of the product was by producing cookbooks featuring Highlander milk recipes. These were extremely popular with housewives the country over and are now quite collectable.

The year 1915 saw the formation of a company called New Zealand Milk Products. They bought out Murrays but continued to manufacture Highlander at Underwood. The endless uses of condensed milk continue to be espoused, including eating it on bread like jam and using it to make any number of sweet treats from ice cream to hot chocolate to cake icing.

Ownership of Highlander remained with New Zealand Milk Products until it was bought out by the current owners, Nestlé, in 1938. They ceased production at Underwood in 1964 and the site is now home to a thriving Sunday market.

Chesdale cheese

Those boys from down on the farm who really know their cheese, Ches and Dale were lunchbox favourites around the country for many years. It's hard to think about Chesdale cheese without picturing the two all-singing all-dancing dairy-farming mascots. So popular were they that there's even a tallish tale that when a New Zealand trade delegation overseas were asked to sing a New Zealand folk song, the Chesdale tune was the only one they all knew!

Before the advent of supermarkets and vacuum-packed blocks of cheese, you used to have to buy your cheese at the local shop. There they'd have huge big wheels of cheese from which they'd cut you a chunk. There weren't any fridges or GLAD Wrap so the cheese would be a bit hard on the outside and, if you were unlucky, the same on the inside.

This got Jack Butland of Butland Industries thinking. He reckoned that if there was some way to process good cheese so that it would keep without going hard or mouldy then Kiwis would buy it. After a bit of experimenting he found that by adding small amounts of chemicals like sodium to the cheese and whipping it a bit you could make the cheese go the texture of smooth peanut butter. It could then be wrapped in aluminium foil and it wouldn't go off. He was onto a good thing!

By the end of the 1960s, though, people had fridges, they could buy smaller blocks of cheese and they started to wonder what was in the processed cheese. Enter Ches and Dale. The two friendly farmers persuaded us that Chesdale cheese was the 'finest cheddar', nothing more, nothing less.

Ches and Dale's legendary song was written in 1968 by Terry Gray, with lyrics by Robert Jenkins. The jingle was then recorded by an Auckland folk group, the Yeomen, which consisted of Brian Borland, Peter Carter and Gordon Hubbard. Rumour has it that when they recorded the song they ad-libbed an extra line that might not have

MADE IN NEW ZEALAND

thrilled the advertisers — 'Finest Colby, gone mouldy!'

Of course, the jingle would be nothing without the drawings of Ches and Dale. These were originally done by Don Couldrey in the early 1960s. But when the boys needed to 'go live' for the telly in 1968 a company called Sam Harvey Animations was hired to do the job. On the animation team for the boys were the famous New Zealand artist Dick Frizzell and legendary animator (and one of the team behind Kapai the Kiwi) John Ewing.

The Ches and Dale television ads continued until about 1975 but live on through that catchy little song. They had done their job well, and Chesdale sales boomed throughout the decade — with the cheese being sold in blocks, segments and individually wrapped slices.

Edmonds

There's nothing like the taste of home baking. Think about it — what were your favourites when you were a kid? Afghans, Melting Moments, Anzac biscuits, Belgian biscuits, chocolate fudge or a good old cornflour sponge? Chances are that whoever baked these for you was the proud owner of the classic New Zealand *Edmonds Cookery Book*.

The Edmonds story started not with the cookbook, but with home cooks in Christchurch complaining about the cruddy quality of baking powder being imported in the 1870s. A 20-year-old Englishman who had just arrived in the country and set up a grocery store took notice of his customers' complaints and decided to do something about it.

Thomas Edmonds had worked for a confectioner back in England, and one of the products he'd learned to make there was sherbet. That fizzy favourite was made from bicarbonate of soda, cream of tartar, sugar and flavouring. Funnily enough, baking powder is made by mixing bicarbonate of soda and cream of tartar, so Edmonds reckoned he might just be able to brew up some baking powder for the local market. He set to work in a room at the back of his shop and came up with a reliable recipe.

Despite all their complaining, it was a while before Christchurch customers would believe that Edmonds' new baking powder was any good. In fact, when one woman challenged him, asking whether his new product was going to work, Edmonds responded, 'Madam, it's sure to rise!' Sound familiar? It should. Edmonds realised that 'Sure to Rise' was the ideal catchcry for his product and it soon became his trademark.

Business was pretty slow for Edmonds to start with, but he used some impressive marketing ploys to get people to buy his baking powder. He gave away 200 samples around his neighbourhood so that the locals all knew about it. He then began to take the baking powder further afield, offering it to people to try, and saying that if they didn't like it they could just give it back next time he came to visit. Word is that he never had any given back!

One of Edmonds' best marketing tools made its first outing in 1907. The very first Edmonds cookbook was a small 50-page leaflet of economical recipes featuring Edmonds products. The value of the book soon became evident, and it grew in size and popularity. Soon it was being sent out to all newly engaged couples in the country so that the little wifey would be able to have a hearty meal on the table when hubby got home!

The first glossy-covered edition of the book appeared in 1955,

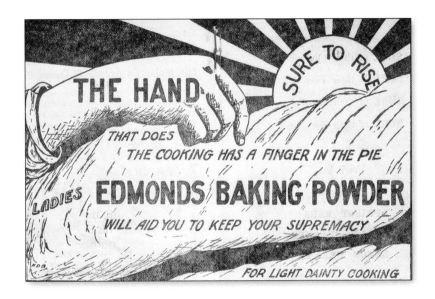

THE HAND THAT DOES THE COOKING HAS A FINGER IN THE PIE

LADIES EDMONDS BAKING POWDER WILL AID YOU TO KEEP YOUR SUPREMACY

SURE TO RISE

FOR LIGHT DAINTY COOKING

and it has continued to change with the times ever since. It no longer has a section entitled 'Invalids', which used to have alarmingly bland recipes in it for sick people, and it now makes allowances for the popularity of the microwave. Nearly four million Edmonds cookbooks have been sold over the years, making it one of this country's best-selling (and best-loved) cookbooks.

As for Thomas Edmond, he retired from the company in 1911. He did, however, oversee the building of the iconic Edmonds factory in 1920. The building can now only be seen on Edmonds packets, as it was controversially demolished in 1990. The gardens around the old factory, however, are open to the public and maintained by the Christchurch City Council.

Thomas Edmond died in 1932 but his legacy lives on in Edmonds products, cookbooks and gardens.

Griffin's

When John Griffin, his wife and their seven children arrived in New Zealand from the Isle of Wight, it's hardly surprising that he set up his own food business. Let's face it, if you're feeding a family of nine, what's a few more mouths to feed?

Seriously though, when the Griffin family arrived in Nelson in May 1854, they initially lived out in the backblocks on a farm. After about ten years Griffin moved the tribe into town and set up a business milling flour and cocoa.

With a huge supply of flour and cocoa on his hands, what else was he going to do but start making biscuits and lollies and other sweet treats? OK, he also sold coal and wood, but it doesn't really fit with the biscuit thing, does it?

From the mid-1860s until the 1890s the Griffin family food business ticked along quite nicely, until one fateful day in 1895. There was a huge fire (and a lot of burnt biscuits) and John Griffin's factory was burnt to the ground. Even though business had been quite good he couldn't afford to rebuild the factory, so he sought shareholders. The resulting company was called Griffin & Sons Ltd.

They say lightning doesn't strike twice but when you're in the business of baking, fire certainly can. In 1903 the rebuilt factory burnt down again. Having learned a few lessons on the fire front, Griffin's built their new factory out of brick instead of wood. They also had to raise more money and get more shareholders on board.

It was another 35 years before Griffin's needed a new factory — and this time it wasn't because the old one had burnt down. No, business was so good that they decided to build a brand new factory in Lower Hutt. John Griffin's grandson Charles moved across Cook Strait with the factory — not for sentimental reasons, but because he was now the boss at Griffin's.

By the time the new factory opened in 1938 Griffin's was already making some of the treats that we still love today — Gingernuts (accept no imitation, if they don't hurt your teeth a little bit then they're not the real thing!), Chocolate Wheatens and the famous Wine biscuit range — Round Wines, Super Wines and Vanilla Wines.

Intriguingly, there are a couple of different tales about the origins of Wine biscuits, and neither of them is about their being as sweet as the wine made in this country at the time. One story is that the flour used to bake Wine biscuits was packed into old wine barrels for transportation. The other is that the Griffins brought the recipe for Wine biscuits from Europe, where it was customary to serve them with wine. The real story — who knows?

Eta

Eta might have one of the shortest names of all New Zealand brands, but it's got a story that's a whole lot bigger than its name. The company's history starts in Australia in 1949, but don't worry, it doesn't stay there for long!

A company with the vaguely amusing name of Nut Food Propriety Limited was in business across the Tasman. In 1949 the Nut Food folk decided they wanted to start a company on this side of the ditch. That company was called Eta Foods. That's Eta as in 'Eat A', not Eta as in ETA, the Basque separatist movement.

Their first factory was in Kingdon St, in the middle of Auckland's now-fashionable Newmarket — it was just around the corner from the Lion Brewery, which was handy for anyone who liked a packet of peanuts with their beer!

Although they started out producing nut products with the catchy tagline 'Eat A Nut', Eta soon diversified to produce potato chips too (oh and peanut butter, mayonnaise, mustard and cooking oil . . . but it's the snack food you're interested in, right?).

Within five or six years Eta employed 50 people and had three salesmen driving around in vans making sure their product got into dairies around Auckland. A key marketing ploy used by Eta was to give away their fine products at events. Lots of Aucklanders would have tried their first Eta chips or nuts for free at the Easter Show — and a few probably disposed of them not long afterwards on the Hurricane or some such similar ride!

The Eta brand became so popular that it soon outgrew its Newmarket premises and the company moved its production to a site in the Auckland suburb of Wiri, where they opened a new plant in 1971. This gave the company the chance to put in new technology that enabled them to use two layers of cellophane in their chip bags.

The company expanded further in the 1980s. In 1982 Eta bought the Dunedin-based chip company Jacks (who made THE best cheese and onion chips ever). Jacks was also the maker of Munchos, a brand of snack that Eta continues to make, although not in all the flavours Jacks did — Marmite, and cheese and pineapple, being two of the casualties!

A couple of years later, Eta acquired the Palmerston North-based Chippies brand from Cadbury's. Chippies is probably best remembered for its triple pack, which went down well right across the lower North Island.

These acquisitions made Eta one of the two biggest snackfood companies in the country, along with Bluebird. With Jacks and Chippies gone, the Eta Ripple reigned supreme!

Whittaker's

If customs officers at London's Heathrow airport were allowed to confiscate chocolate it wouldn't take them long to build up a lifetime supply of Whittaker's Peanut Slabs. They're one of those legendary products that Kiwis on their OE hanker for when they're living overseas. There are flats in London that charge recently arrived dossers by the night — in Peanut Slabs. The most I've ever imported into the UK is 40, and that was only for my brother, my sister and my cousin (who's not even a Kiwi!).

The magic that is the Peanut Slab arrived on the scene in this country in the 1950s, but the Whittakers had been making chocolate long before they started adding peanuts to it. James Henry Whittaker was brought up in Macclesfield in England, where at the age of 14 he started work for a confectioner.

He arrived in New Zealand in 1890 and initially settled in Christchurch. It was there, in 1896, that he established Whittaker's confectionary from a small factory in the backyard of his home in Addington. As the business was small he had to make all the product himself, then ride around on his horse visiting stockists and selling it as well.

After 17 years in Christchurch he decided to move the business to Wellington, establishing a factory in the central city. Around this time he also brought his sons James and Ronald into partnership with him, and the name of the business was officially changed to JH Whittaker & Sons.

Business was good in this new setting and the Whittaker name became known for producing good quality sweets at affordable prices — something that had been James Whittaker's aim from the outset.

After 20 years in Wellington, the Whittakers registered the business as a limited liability company, retaining all the shares within the family. Unusually in a time of megaconglomerates, the company remains solely in the Whittaker family's hands today, albeit in the hands of the third generation of Whittakers!

It was in the early 1950s that a traditional way of selling chocolate led to the invention of Whittaker's best-selling bar — the good old Peanut Slab. They were inspired by the way chocolate used to be sold to shopkeepers in massive 2.25-kilogram blocks. The shopkeeper would then chop off slabs of chocolate for customers and charge them for it by weight. Whittaker's came up with the idea of adding peanuts to chocolate and selling it in smaller slabs that were reminiscent of the giant blocks of old. Boxes of these slabs were placed on the counters of grocery stores, encouraging people to make a last-minute impulse buy — the grocer popping the chocolate bar in a paper bag for the customer to munch on on the way home.

It wasn't until 1984 that Whittaker's began selling the wrapped bars that you see in most supermarkets today. They also started selling 250-gram Peanut Blocks around that time, to cater for those people for whom a 50-gram block just wasn't enough!

As well as Peanut Slabs, Whittaker's make another one of New Zealand's favourite sweets – the K-Bar. These wee fruit flavoured toffee bars were originally called Kwench Bars but the Whittakers thought that name was too long for a small bar so they just cut the name down to K-Bar.

In 1969, the company moved to the Porirua factory where they continue to make chocolate and sweets today.

Eskimo Pies

Being the biggest ice cream eaters in the world, Kiwis have heaps of choice when it comes to their favourite iced confections. But there's one type of ice cream we've taken to so much that it will be eligible for superannuation soon — the Eskimo Pie.

Eskimo Pies haven't changed much over their long life. They've always been made of vanilla ice cream, coated in chocolate and wrapped in foil. The thing that sets Eskimo Pies apart from other ice creams is that they have never had a stick or a cone. They're so tempting that you just wrap your hands around the Eskimo Pie and devour it so quickly you don't have to worry about it melting.

In the early 1950s the people charged with developing new ice cream flavours at Tip Top decided to start making some single-serve ice cream treats. This meant that not all ice cream would have to be rolled and put in a cone, saving ice cream sellers time. It was also hoped that the novelty value of the new ice cream would increase ice cream sales.

Like many manufacturers in New Zealand in the 1950s, Tip Top looked to the United States for inspiration and there they found their new product: the Eskimo Pie.

Eskimo Pies were first produced in a town called Onawa, in Iowa, in 1920. Apparently a sweetshop owner there, Christian Nelson, was serving a young customer in his store. The boy was spending absolutely ages trying to make up his mind whether to buy an ice cream or a chocolate bar. Nelson suggested that he should just buy both. The boy told him he'd love to buy both of them — but he only had enough money for one.

While most people wouldn't give something like this a second thought, it bugged Nelson. He got to thinking about whether it would be possible to combine chocolate and ice cream so that his customers would get more bang for their buck. He experimented for weeks trying to make chocolate stick to ice cream, until eventually he realised that cocoa butter was the key to getting the two sweet treats to stick together.

Once he'd got that sussed he set about making the ice cream

chocolate bars, marketing them as I-Scream bars. Shortly after, he made a deal with an ice cream manufacturer, Russell Stover, to make the bars in bulk, and this is when the name was changed. Nelson and Stover agreed the product needed a name change, and Mrs Stover suggested Eskimo Pie. The product was such a hit that by 1922 a million Eskimo Pies were being sold every day in America! The pair were initially granted a patent for their new product but this was later withdrawn, much to the relief of ice cream makers the world over!

While the Eskimo Pie hasn't changed much since its introduction in New Zealand in the 1950s, attitudes to indigenous populations have — it's hard to imagine anyone getting away with calling a product Eskimo Pie today! The term Eskimo is no longer used to describe a people (in fact, it can be seen as quite offensive) and indigenous populations of Canada, Alaska and Greenland are now known as Inuit peoples.

ON THE
MAP

2

Most Kiwi businesses start pretty small, but before long some of them become so important to the towns where they are based that the company name and the town are inextricably linked. Here are just a few of the companies that have helped put their towns on the map.

Yarrows Family Bakers

Wellington's stadium might have earned itself the nickname Cake Tin, but surely it would be more appropriate for New Plymouth's stadium to be called the Bread Basket. Why? Well, the stadium's actual name is Yarrow Stadium, and it — like many of the teams who play there — is sponsored by the company that has put the town of Manaia on the map — Yarrows Family Bakers.

Manaia is to be found between Hawera and Opunake in South Taranaki — you can't miss it, it's the one with the huge loaf of bread taking pride of place on the main street. It's a small town that's home to a family company that has been baking bread since 1923. The relationship between the town and the company is so strong that about a quarter of Manaia's 1000 inhabitants have jobs at Yarrows.

The fact that this small-town, family-run company has lasted so long is pretty amazing, but even more amazing is that their products aren't just destined for Taranaki toasters — they're eaten all over New Zealand, Australia, Taiwan, Japan, Singapore, Korea . . . the list goes on!

The Yarrow link with Manaia started in 1923 when Grace and Alfred Yarrow moved into town and bought the local bakery. Not only did they bake bread and cakes, but the family also ran a teashop and did local catering. Living out the back of the shop meant that all four of the Yarrows' children, Joyce, Berriss, Hec and Noel, got involved in the business at an early age.

The business thrived and Alf started a Yarrow family tradition of giving back to the community. Before long he was a JP and a town board member.

While stock and labour shortages caused many small-town businesses to falter during the Second World War, Yarrows managed to tough it out. Times were hard, but Alf Yarrow knew that the way to survive tough times was to be innovative. He invested in labour-saving technology and ensured that the company stayed ahead of its competitors.

Following Alf's sudden death in 1952, his sons Hec and Noel took over running the business. Alf's innovative nature had rubbed off on his sons, and over the years they continued to look overseas for new ideas, technology and expertise. Yarrows continued to grow — expanding from being a town bakery to a Taranaki bakery and then a global bakery. Sadly, Noel passed away in April 2008 at the age of 83, but the family business continues.

You might not know it but every Subway sandwich you eat will have started its life at Yarrows in Manaia. Ever since the chain arrived in New Zealand in 1996, Yarrows has been supplying them with bread dough. The company was so impressed with the product that Yarrows bread is now being munched by Subway lovers in Japan, Korea, Taiwan and Australia. That's a lot of bread! The company also exports croissants, rolls, pastries and breads to other parts of the world. And the good news is that we don't have to go overseas to get our hands on the good stuff!

Temuka pottery

It seems almost predestined that Temuka would be the home of one of New Zealand's most famous pottery companies. After all, the town's name is a corruption of the Maori phrase Te Umu Kaha, which means the fierce earth oven. Local Maori used to build big ovens in the ground to roast the roots of cabbage trees. But today the fierce ovens could easily be taken to mean the pottery kilns that have put the town's name on dinner tables and in china cabinets throughout the country.

The Temuka Homewares story started almost by accident in the early 1930s. Temuka had been home to a company making porcelain electrical insulators from local clay since 1918. In the 1930s the manager of the National Electric and Engineering Company factory, Arthur Toplis, realised that the company had everything they needed to make Christmas presents for their customers, so he set about getting some small tobacco jars and ashtrays made.

The company's customers must have thought these little knick-knacks were an improvement on the usual calendar or box of biscuits, and Toplis's range of giftware expanded to include vases and teapots. Eventually the owners of the electrical company realised that Toplis's sideline could be a money-spinner, and began to develop the pottery range further. One of their top ranges combined the expertise of the potters and the electrical experts. Temuka began to supply the bodies of electric jugs to a number of manufacturers around the country.

With the onset of the Second World War, the Temuka production line focused on making practical products — even supplying teapots to the Indian army. They must have been sturdy teapots, as just after the war ended Temuka got the contract to make tea cups and saucers for New Zealand Railways. Probably the most famous product to come from Temuka, the Railways cup was thought to be almost unbreakable!

Things then went a bit quiet on the pottery front at Temuka — that was until the 1970s hit. The must-have homeware buy of the decade became Temuka Stoneware. And buy it we did. New Zealanders went mad for the range, which included dinner sets, coffee sets, tea sets, casseroles, storage jars . . . you name it. All this stoneware came in any shade, so long as it was brown.

A decade later and Kiwis were pretty much over their obsession with brown homewares. The eighties were all about colour (heck, it was the decade of the bright blue eye shadow, eyeliner, handbag and shoes!). Temuka followed fashion and started to introduce a broader range of homewares in different shapes, patterns and colours. It's a trend that continues to this day, with a huge range of brightly coloured Temuka homeware. But there are still those who hanker after a bit of brown, and the earlier Temuka ware is now a popular collectors' item.

Lemon and Paeroa

Lemon and Te Aroha, Wai Ronga, Wai Aroha . . . these were all mineral waters marketed in the early 1900s, and they could have become 'world famous in New Zealand'. But they didn't, because Kiwis fell in love with what we now know as L&P — Lemon and Paeroa.

The small town of Paeroa near the Firth of Thames is home to about 4000 people and one big reputation! The L&P story goes back to the early Maori inhabitants of the area, who were the first to discover springs of mineral water bubbling from the ground. When gold was struck on the Coromandel in the 1860s the miners who crowded to the region would seek out the water the morning after they'd been on a boozy bender.

The tales of fizzy water bubbling from the ground attracted the government balneologist — yep, they had their own mineral-water expert! — Arthur Wohlman. He began studying the Paeroa water in 1904. What he found was 'a large warm effervescing spring . . . containing 73 grains of magnesium bicarbonate to the gallon'. He reckoned the water was pleasant to drink and 'good for dyspepsia', adding 'it can be beneficial for constipation'. He might have been right about that, but he got it a bit wrong when he said he reckoned New Zealanders drank so much tea they probably wouldn't go to the expense of bottling the water!

Local people would walk to the spring, have a drink there (sometimes adding a little lemon to the water) then fill a few bottles to take home. In 1908 Robert Fewell and Frank Brinkler bought the property the spring was on, and started bottling and selling it through the Paeroa Natural Mineral Water Company.

In 1915, they sold the company to Menzies and Company. They then began to market the water mixed with lemon juice, calling it Paeroa and Lemon. By 1926 demand for the water was so high that a new factory was opened in Paeroa. Demand for the flavoured beverage was so strong that water was being shipped to Auckland so that it could be mixed there for the local market.

It's not really clear when the name got flipped around but in the late 1940s both 'Paeroa and Lemon' and 'Lemon and Paeroa' were being used. In 1963, Menzies and Co merged with CL Innes, a Hamilton company that had manufactured Lemon and Te Aroha. That was when L&P took on the distinctive Innes tartan, which graced its labels until the late 1970s when Oasis Industries took over the company. Oasis was then taken over by Coca Cola, and L&P is now produced by the world's biggest fizz-makers.

The Paeroa factory was eventually closed in 1980, so L&P doesn't actually have Paeroa's famous water in it any more. However, Arthur Wohlman's early mineral analysis provided a recipe so that L&P's makers are able to replicate the water, ensuring that famous L&P taste lives on.

Barker's of Geraldine

There's a little shop in the Four Peaks Plaza in Geraldine that attracts an incredible 70,000 visitors a year and it's not just because they make a mean boysenberry smoothie! The shop is the hometown retail outlet of Geraldine's most famous export, Barker's. The Barker's name has become as synonymous with the town of Geraldine as it has with the production of quality fruit products.

Barker's is a family-owned company that employs about 120 people in Geraldine making more than 500 products. And it all started with a bottle of elderberry wine — that's right, elderberry wine!

New Zealand might be world famous for its wine now, but back in the 1960s the wine produced in this country was . . . well . . . the politest word for it is probably — ordinary. Import tariffs meant that bringing wine in from overseas was really expensive. So the good old

41
On the map

Kiwi innovation came into play, and lots of people used to make their own wine with whatever fruit they had.

Anthony Barker was certainly one of these innovative Kiwis (he also invented the famous Kent log fire). In 1969, he used some local Geraldine elderberries to make a batch of fruit wine. When it came time to taste it, he and his wife Gillian realised that it was not only drinkable, it was really good! They decided they could be on to something, and they started to make small batches of fruit wines and liqueurs for the local market.

A glut of high-quality blackcurrants in the South Canterbury area led the Barkers to thinking about how they could use all the excess fruit. They decided to make it into syrup which could be bottled and then used in a number of different ways, including as a base for a fruit drink. Thanks to that abundance of blackcurrants, Barker's blackcurrant syrup remains their most popular product today.

To make the syrup, the Barkers had to build a processing factory on the family farm. Once they had the processing factory it made sense to branch out and try other things — plenty of other things! They now make jams, chutneys, sauces, preserves, drink concentrates . . . you name it.

When Anthony Barker passed away in 1999, his son Michael took over the reins of the business. He continues his father's legacy of using high-quality fresh produce in all of their lines — so much so that Barker's now uses over 500 tonnes of fresh fruit every year, sourcing as much of it as possible from New Zealand growers.

The best of Geraldine can now be found not only in shops in New Zealand but also in Australia, Canada, Taiwan and Japan. But not the boysenberry smoothies — you've still got to go to Geraldine for those!

Glaxo

It may come as a surprise to know that one of the world's largest pharmaceutical companies had its humble beginning in a dairy factory in the town of Bunnythorpe, near Palmerston North. It's true though, Glaxo SmithKline — which now employs more than 100,000 people in 100 countries, making such well-known products as Lucozade, Panadol and Sensodyne — started life in little old Bunnythorpe in 1906.

The man behind what is now a massive international brand was Joseph Nathan. Born in the East End of London in 1835, Nathan emigrated to Australia in 1853. After working in Melbourne for four years he made the move across the Tasman and into the pages of history.

On his arrival in Wellington, Nathan went to work with his brother-in-law, Jacob Joseph, in Jacob's importing company. He was soon made a partner in the company, and used his share of the profits to invest in land that was just being opened up to the north. By 1867, Joseph Nathan owned a large chunk of land in the Manawatu.

In 1873, Nathan took over the whole company and renamed it Joseph Nathan and Co. His sons worked with him as he continued to build the business. Nathan was always interested in new technology — he was involved in some of the earliest exports of frozen meat, and the development of rail from Wellington to Manawatu.

This interest in technology met Nathan's investment in the Manawatu when the family company negotiated the rights to manufacture dried milk in New Zealand in the early 1900s. The company owned 17 creameries in the Manawatu so it made sense for the milk processing to be done there. In 1904, the Nathans built a dried-milk factory in Bunnythorpe.

Although the Nathan link with Bunnythorpe started in 1904, the Glaxo name hadn't yet come into being. The dried milk produced there was branded Defiance. The brand name was perhaps the Nathans' way of letting people know they wouldn't be bullied — in its first year of production an attempt had been made to burn down the factory and then blow it up!

While it might have scared off would-be saboteurs, Defiance wasn't a very appealing name for potential milk buyers, so the Nathans decided they needed a new name for their product. Initially they were going to call it Lacto but there were already products available with a similar name, so it was back to the drawing board. They mucked around with the letters in the name and tried to come up with something a bit more catchy, and thus Glaxo was born. The name was registered in October 1906. Joseph Nathan died in 1912 but the company he had started lived on.

The Nathans began exporting Glaxo to England, where they used the slogan 'Glaxo builds bonnie babies'. The promotion of Glaxo milk as a baby formula, and its use by soldiers in the First World War, established the Glaxo name in the British market. By 1925 the brand was so ensconced in the British market that it even got a mention in Virginia Woolf's novel *Mrs Dalloway*.

Since then the Glaxo company has continued to grow and change. It is now a massive international conglomerate producing four billion packets of medicine and health products a year. Even though the Bunnythorpe factory closed in 1974, the town will always be the home of Glaxo.

Norsewear

When the ship *Hovding* arrived at Napier on 15 September 1872, it carried 372 Norwegians and 11 Swedes (being people from Sweden, not the turnip-like vegetables). These intrepid Scandinavian settlers soon founded their own town in dense forest in Hawke's Bay. The name of that town? Norsewood. Norse meaning Norwegian and wood, well, that's self-explanatory!

Since the late 1960s the town's name has become almost synonymous with a business that made its name in Norsewood — Norsewear. But the Norsewear story started a while before the company did.

Born and brought up in Norway, Ola Rian loved the outdoors. After spending some time in the Norwegian army, he decided it was time to see the world. He'd heard there was some great skiing to be had in New Zealand, so he headed south to see our great outdoors. You know how the story goes . . . he liked it so much, he stayed!

Ola and his wife Shirley settled in Wellington, but they spent heaps of time in the mountains. After a few ski trips they realised there was a market for good quality woollen ski-wear — back in the days when you didn't need a degree in chemistry to understand what your ski gear was made of! In 1963, the Rians invested in a knitting machine and started making hats and socks especially for the ski market. They called their company Norsewear Homecrafts in recognition of Ola's homeland, and right from the start they used the distinctive Norsewear snowflake as their company logo.

Ola Rian combined his work in the company with the role of Norwegian Consul General in this country. As such, he was invited to attend the celebrations of some descendants of the original Norwegian settlers in . . . yep . . . Norsewood. And for the second time in his life, he liked it so much he stayed.

The Rians had been talking about expanding the business, and they decided that Norsewood was the ideal place to do it. They established the Norsewear factory there in the late 1960s, employing local people to produce the heavy flecked socks and jerseys that the company has become so famous for. Norsewear's reputation for being hardwearing and warm has seen the products worn by the New Zealand army and Kiwi reps living at Scott Base in Antarctica.

The company has gone through a number of ownership changes since its inception and its head office is now based in Auckland. Even if Norsewear isn't made in Norsewood any more (or even, indeed, in New Zealand) the town and the company will always be inextricably linked in the minds of many Kiwis.

Wattie's

It's hard to imagine life without Wattie's — no wee sachets of Wattie's tomato sauce to go with your fish 'n' chips, no big bottles of Wattie's barbecue sauce to go with your burnt snarlers at a barbecue, no Wattie's baked beans for those slow-start Saturday mornings, no Wattie's frozen peas to go on that sprained ankle . . . In the years since the company began, Wattie's has become a truly national brand — but there's one place that has more claim to it than the rest of us, and that's Hastings.

The Wattie's link with Hastings goes back to the early 1900s.

On the map

Although the company's founder, James Wattie, was born in Canterbury and had his early schooling in Marlborough, his family moved to Hawke's Bay in time for him to pass his standard six proficiency exam at Mahora South School. Even though he was only 13, he had already had several jobs before he became a junior clerk at the Hawke's Bay Farmers' Meat Company, where he stayed for five years while also studying accounting by correspondence.

By 1928 he was the manager of Hawke's Bay Fruitgrowers. At that time, growers in the region were supplying whole fruit for export, and surplus fruit was left to rot on the ground rather than being used for jam, pulp or canning. In 1934 Wattie heard from an accountant friend, Harold Carr, that despite all the local fruit being left to rot, an Auckland company was looking at importing fruit pulp from Tasmania to make jam. Wattie contacted the company, and soon the two men had landed an order for Hawke's Bay fruit to replace the Australian supply.

This left them with a bit of a problem. Wattie and Carr needed to build a processing plant for the fruit. Hawke's Bay Fruitgrowers didn't have the cash to get into the pulp business, but they backed the two men with a plan to sell bonds to raise the money required. It took only two days before they had the money they needed!

Within a very short time they had installed the machinery they needed in a rented cottage and delivered their first load of jam pulp to Auckland. Now they had the gear to process fruit, Wattie and Carr diversified and started to can peaches and pears too. Hawke's Bay being one of New Zealand's biggest fruit-growing regions, raw product wasn't hard to come by.

By the end of 1935 Wattie and Carr were so successful that they took over land and buildings from Hawke's Bay Fruitgrowers and registered their new company — J Wattie Canneries. This was the start of what was to become Hawke's Bay's biggest business.

When a massive frost hit the nearby Heretaunga Plains in 1936, Wattie thought on his feet. What could they do if they had no fruit? They did some experiments with tinning asparagus and peas, then hit upon a product that would see them through some tough times — tinned tomatoes.

Before long, J Wattie Canneries had contracts to supply 50,000 cases of canned goods a year to Kiwi wholesalers. This helped fund the building of a whole new factory, and increased the supply of fruit and vegetables from local growers. The future of Wattie's had been assured.

Now owned by the American-based HJ Heinz Company, Wattie's employs nearly 2000 people at its two factories in Hastings, one on the original King St site and one at Tomoana, and its factory in Christchurch.

Jimmy's Pies

There's a Southlander living in Auckland — who may or may not be the author of this book — who is so enamoured of Jimmy's fine products that she'll try and talk anyone making the trip north to pop a few in their hand luggage, much to the entertainment of the handbag-scanning guys at airports around the South Island!

While you can find Jimmy's Pies in dairies, supermarkets and cafes around the lower half of the South Island, there's nothing like buying

"DELICIOUS EATEN HOT OR COLD"

Quality Goods From

"Jimmy's"

MINCE PIE

Manufactured by JIMMY'S PIES LTD.
143 Scotland St, Roxburgh
New Zealand

one in the very place they're made — Roxburgh. In fact, Jimmy's Pies have become so famous that plenty of people make the pilgrimage to Roxburgh every year just to visit the source.

The relationship between Jimmy's and Roxburgh goes back to the early 1960s. The company's founder and the original Jimmy, Jimmy

Kirkpatrick, had initially owned a bakery in Invercargill. But he moved the company to open a bakehouse in Roxburgh at the same time the hydro dam was being built on the Clutha River — all those hungry workers loved Jimmy's Pies.

Starting with just four staff, Jimmy produced pies to an old Scottish recipe that he'd been given by a Scotsman called Herbert Stott. The same recipe is still in use today — it's that good. While many pie companies make their money from their fancy gourmet pies, Jimmy's main business is in traditional pie flavours — mince, mince and cheese, bacon and egg, and that Southern favourite, mutton.

When Jimmy died in 1976, his son Dennis decided to leave his banking career in Wellington and move back to Roxburgh and the company business. When Dennis took over, Jimmy's was making about 1200 pies a day. Plenty to keep a small-town bakery going — but Dennis had other ideas. In the time he's been running the company, he's invested in new equipment, expanded the Jimmy's range and employed more people.

Jimmy's now has about 30 staff and they make a massive 20,000 pies a day, which are all then packed into the company's trademark paper bags. Business is so good that the wee Jimmy's Pie shop on Roxburgh's main street has undergone a huge makeover without missing out on baking a single pie — they just packed up and moved down the road a bit while the building work went on. Which has got to be a good thing, as there'd be many a road trip, hangover, airport wait and hastily grabbed lunch that would be much less bearable if Jimmy's ever stopped making its pies.

WEARABLE WONDERS

3

New Zealand and fashion haven't always been
terms that sit easily together. What we are good
at is making stuff that's practical, hard-wearing
and comfortable. After all, where would the
country be without its Red Bands, Swanndris,
Jandals and the like?

Hallensteins

Girlfriends and wives have been dragging their men to Hallensteins to be kitted out for more than 130 years. The chain of menswear stores has become a New Zealand institution in a country where for a long time men would rather go nude than go shopping.

The Hallensteins story started back with the birth of the unusually named Bendix Hallenstein in Germany in 1835. Bendix's parents ran a mill where they made clothes from rags, but Bendix was the youngest in the family, so he wasn't going to be taking over the family business. Instead he moved to Manchester in England at the age of 17. Manchester didn't really do it for him so after five years there he joined two of his brothers, Isaac and Michaelis, in Australia. Guess what they were doing there? Yep, they were following the gold rushes. They all pitched up at Daylesford, in Victoria, in 1857.

The Hallenstein brothers ran a store in the town selling supplies to miners. The business nearly turned to custard when all three of the brothers set their caps after the same woman — their housekeeper, Mary Mountain. In a scene straight from a Hollywood movie, Bendix won Mary's heart, and the pair went back to England to marry in 1861 (possibly to get away from Bendix's jilted brothers!).

Two years after their marriage, Bendix and Mary (and the other Hallenstein brothers) followed another gold rush and came to New Zealand. They opened a store in Invercargill but the lure of blue cod and oysters wasn't enough to keep them there. Eventually Bendix moved up the line, closer to the action in Queenstown, where he opened another store, selling everything from food and wine to clothes and ironware. The store was a real success, and soon after,

Hallenstein opened stores in other gold towns around the region — Arrowtown, Lawrence and Cromwell.

Evidence of Hallenstein's time in Queenstown can still be seen (but get there quick before they pull it down and build more apartments) in the old stone courthouse that he commissioned as mayor. The remains of the grand homestead he built, Thurlby Domain, still stand near present-day Millbrook.

Despite his long-term link with Queenstown, it was in Dunedin that Hallenstein first got involved in clothing manufacture. Supplying miners throughout Central Otago, Hallenstein soon realised that good quality men's clothing was hard to come by. In 1873 he established New Zealand's first clothing factory in Dunedin, but financial troubles meant he soon had to sell it. He leased the factory back, though, and started making ready-to-wear men's clothes using fabric made at the local Roslyn and Mosgiel woollen mills.

A year later the first Hallensteins menswear store opened in the Octagon in Dunedin, and it was a hit. Within 25 years there were 34 Hallensteins stores selling men's clothing throughout the country. The success of the company saw Hallenstein and his family move to Dunedin, where he also established the Drapery and General Importing Company — which you may know as the now-defunct department store chain, DIC.

Bendix Hallenstein retained control of the company until his death in 1905. The following year it became a limited liability company. At its peak in 1986 there were 72 Hallensteins stores around the country, although since then they have been consolidated around the main centres. In 1987 Hallensteins merged with Glassons, making it this country's biggest clothing company.

Jandals

It's been said that the true test of whether you're a Kiwi or not is how you would answer the following question:

Where would you wear a thong?

Of course, for real Kiwis the thong is a small piece of underwear that is never worn on the feet. In other countries flip-flops might be called thongs, but in this country they're Jandals all the way!

The history of the Jandal is a disputed one. One version of the story says that Morris Yock was working as a sales representative for his grandfather's company in Asia when he came across locals wearing a funny sandal that was just a sole with straps running from either side, joining between the toe. He asked around and was told they were Japanese sandals.

Yock thought these sandals were pretty cool, and he reckoned they might go down a treat with beach-going, outdoor-loving New Zealanders. Typically, Yock started making these sandals in his garage, and in 1957 the Jandal trademark was registered and the product hit the market. Jandal is a combination of Japanese and sandal.

In typical flowery New Zealand bloke style Yock called the manufacturing company Jandals Limited. And limited they were — to brown and white. Coloured jandals arrived a couple of years later.

Yock's first Jandals were made out of rubber sheets imported from Hong Kong. During the 1950s and 60s importation of foreign-made products was difficult and Yock eventually sold the Jandal business to Skellerup, who have continued making Jandals ever since.

The other version of the Jandal story has emerged more recently, with Mary Deken saying that it was her father, John Cowie, who invented the Jandal. According to Deken, her father had been manufacturing plastic Japanese sandals in Hong Kong in the late 1940s, and it was he who first supplied Jandals to Morris Yock in 1957. In 1959 the Cowie family moved from Hong Kong to New Zealand, to find Morris Yock selling their dad's invention.

Deken reckoned her dad was a very humble man and wouldn't have realised the significance of his invention.

Regardless of who invented the Jandal, the fact is that Kiwis love them and can't get enough of the simple footwear. Because Skellerup now own the Jandal trademark, no other company is allowed to call their product Jandals — even if that's what we all call them!

Swanndri

You could almost hear the collective intake of breath from New Zealand's farmers when Swanndri announced that they would be working with Auckland fashion designer Karen Walker to create a new look for some of its clothing lines. Long renowned for their 'if it ain't broke don't fix it' philosophy, the daily Swanndri wearers feared that their favourite brand would soon be beseeching them to 'accessorise, accessorise, accessorise'. Equally palpable was the rural relief when Walker's first Swanndri collection was released, modernising but remaining true to the original Swanndri look.

That original look had its beginnings in Taranaki with a man called William Broome. Having arrived in New Zealand and settled in New Plymouth in 1902, 21-year-old Broome went into business as a tailor and textile merchant. Over the next ten years he talked to

MADE IN NEW ZEALAND

plenty of farmers and bushmen, many of whom complained about the lack of warm, dry, all-weather outdoor clothing.

William Broome decided to help them out, and set about developing a bush shirt that would be weatherproof. The shirts were made of thick wool and then weatherproofed using Broome's own secret formula. He first started selling them in 1913, and they soon caught on with the hardy characters around Taranaki.

The name Swanndri was inspired by the way water runs off a swan's feathers, keeping them dry, which was exactly what Broome wanted his shirts to do for their wearers. The company was registered in 1913 and it was around the same time that William Broome designed and registered the Swanndri logo, which remains in use today.

The manufacture of the shirts was a real family affair, with the fabric being cut out and sewn at Broome's tailor's shop on Devon St. Once the shirts had been made they would be taken back to the Broome family home on Doralto Rd. In the backyard there was a huge concrete tub containing the secret weatherproofing formula. The shirts would be soaked in the tub for about two days before they were ready.

The only side effect of this was that the pure wool shirts would shrink from being in liquid for such a long time. This shrinkage couldn't be managed, so two shirts that went into the dip the same size would almost certainly come out different sizes. Because of this, the earliest Swanndris were one size fits all! It wasn't until John McKendrick took over the company in 1955 that this problem was solved with the use of pre-shrunk fabrics.

These early Swanndris were produced in traditional bushman green — they were so spot on for their market that the exact same colour and cut of shirt are still being sold today.

Bendon

While their spokesmodel is one of the world's most famous Australians, this company is fully and firmly Kiwi. After all, Bendon has supported thousands of New Zealanders for more than 60 years! This country's most successful underwear company began in 1947 when two brothers decided that they could improve on the heavy contraptions that passed for women's 'foundation garments' at the time.

Their timing was perfect. During the Second World War, New Zealand women found themselves doing jobs they never expected to do and realised that they were capable of being more than just wives and mothers. With the end of the war came a new sense of freedom and optimism that hadn't been possible during the war. This new freedom coincided with the lifting of clothing rationing in 1947. During the war, new clothes were rationed so that valuable fabrics, especially woollen and silk ones, could be diverted to military uses. Wool was used for uniforms and silk for parachutes.

When Ray Hurley left his post as an officer in the navy, he decided to set up a business with his brother Des. A pattern cutter by trade, Des's experience in the clothing industry was invaluable. The brothers soon set about designing new women's undergarments that were a major departure from the heavy, uncomfortable and restrictive garments of old.

The Hurley brothers did something quite radical — they actually considered the female body, the range of movement the wearer of their product would need, and the comfort of the wearer. Out went the heavy steel and bone structures that were more like feats of engineering than pieces of clothing. In came lighter, more flexible underwear.

The problem of what to call this new underwear was solved when someone suggested they call it exactly what it did. The lingerie they produced was so flexible, it would 'bend on' the wearer's body. And so Bendon was born. The company's new products were well received by New Zealand women.

The next big innovation from Bendon came in 1963. It might seem strange now to think that stretch straps on bras and stretchy fabric for underwear was such a revolutionary idea, but back then it really was a huge thing. Even though the 1960s was the era when Germaine Greer encouraged women the world over to burn their bras, condemning them as a 'ludicrous invention', no one in New Zealand seemed to be taking any notice. In 1964, Bendon's sales topped $1 million for the first time. That's about $35 million nowadays! By 1966 they had blitzed all their competition and Bendon was the main underwear company in the country.

The company was publicly listed in 1982, but this wasn't nearly as interesting as the big move they made in 1990. Bendon joined forces with one of the hottest models in the world at the time (some would say ever!) — the Australian, Elle Macpherson. The Elle Macpherson range saw the brand suddenly appealing to a whole new generation of Bendon buyers. It also helped the company break into the British, US and Canadian markets. But even though it's got an Australian spokesmodel and is popular in heaps of other countries, Bendon will always be a New Zealand favourite.

Skellerup Red Bands

The very first rubber boots were made by indigenous South Americans who realised that if they poured rubber from rubber trees over their feet and lower legs, it would protect them. Farmers and gardeners the country over should be glad that the technology has moved on somewhat since then!

From tipping it straight on to your feet, rubber has gone on to be made into boots — gumboots to be precise. While the invention of the boots is usually credited to Arthur Wellesley, the first Duke of Wellington, he was only half the equation. The shape of the gumboot was his idea, but the ones he had made were of calfskin. It wasn't until a few years later, when Arthur Goodyear developed the technology to vulcanise rubber, that the gumboot was really invented. And no, it's nothing to do with Dr Spock — vulcanisation is a process that makes rubber flexible.

When it comes to gummies in this country, any cocky will tell you there's only one name — Skellerup. And even though they make heaps of different sorts of gumboots, the Red Band is seen as the one true Kiwi gumboot.

The Skellerup name was originally Skjellerup, brought here by Danish Australian George Skjellerup. He opened his first store selling tyres and other rubber products in Christchurch in 1910. This was the country's first Para Rubber store. It wasn't until 1939 that the company diversified and started making footwear — their first product being canvas tennis shoes.

While many industries had to slow production during the Second World War, Skellerup continued to grow. They turned out huge quantities of gas masks and worked hard to develop footwear for New Zealand's armed forces.

It was during this time that the first Skellerup gumboot came out of the vulcaniser at the company's Christchurch factory, on 9 September 1943. But it wasn't a Red Band. The very first Skellerup boot was called a Marathon — a name that lives on in the company's current range of boots.

Skellerup Industries listed on the stock exchange in 1948, and the company began exporting to Australia a couple of years later. George Skjellerup passed away in 1955, and his son Valdemar took over his role as managing director of the company.

It was under Valdemar's reign that the very first Skellerup Red Band was made — on 21 October 1958 to be precise (making it a Libra that will turn 50 on 21 October 2008!). The story behind the name Red Band is as prosaic as they come. It goes like this — the boots have got a big red band round the top — and a red toe, but that's not really relevant here.

The reason Red Bands have become so popular in New Zealand is because they're tough, durable, longlasting and bloody comfortable. And, let's face it, if it weren't for our Red Bands — where would we be?

Canterbury rugby jerseys

When it comes to clothing, New Zealand designers are making some real inroads on the international fashion scene — World, Karen Walker, Zambesi — they're all becoming more recognised overseas. But there's one much more practical clothing label that has got a huge international following, and that's Canterbury. Yep, the rugby jersey guys.

Canterbury gear is sold in South Africa, the United States, Great Britain, Canada, Japan . . . the list goes on. And it's all on the back of that classic Kiwi rugby jersey. The company that first developed the Canterbury rugby jersey — Lane Walker Rudkin — was, unsurprisingly, based in Christchurch.

The company's story goes back to 1880, when Sarah and Alfred Rudkin established a small business making socks and underwear in their Christchurch home. When they had trouble getting a supply of good yarn, they went into business with John Lane and Pringle Walker, who owned a woollen mill in Ashburton. The four of them decided to join forces, and so Lane Walker Rudkin was born in 1904.

The company soon diversified from their socks and jocks start, and began to produce army uniforms, swimsuits and rugby jerseys. The first national rugby team to wear a Lane Walker Rudkin jersey was the mighty Invincibles in 1924 — a team that included the phenomenal George Nepia.

If the jerseys were good enough for the national team, then provincial sides decided they had to have them too. Before long, LWR was kitting out all the first-division rugby teams. The classic rugby jersey design, with the single white loop forming the neck, nearly didn't make it off the drawing board in the 1950s — teams weren't keen on it when it was first proposed by designer Ashley Hanna, but the company persisted. The Canterbury rugby team soon adopted it and the design took off, remaining the standard for the next 50 years.

The Canterbury brand was used for many years on all of LWR's clothing except their underwear (much of which was produced under another iconic Kiwi brand — Jockey). In the late 1970s the company decided to take its rugby gear to the international markets. The classic jersey soon became a must-have sportswear item in the United States.

The company also focused their marketing on rugby-playing countries — and what better sales pitch than the fact that the All Blacks wore them! The export market was so successful that in 1980 a separate arm of the company, Canterbury Apparel, had to be established to cope with it.

Five years later, with sales booming, the classic Canterbury three-kiwi logo made its first outing, largely to identify the jerseys as the real deal and not one of the cheap rip-offs that were starting to make their way onto the market.

Over time the Canterbury business became so big that it bought out the original LWR company, which still manufactures Canterbury jerseys under licence to Canterbury International Ltd. While the Canterbury kiwis are no longer seen opposite the silver fern on All Black jerseys, they still make plenty of outings in international rugby. Canterbury jerseys are worn by such international powerhouses as Australia, Ireland, Scotland, South Africa, Swaziland and Monaco. They can also be seen on both Australian rugby league State of Origin teams, and in 2007 they even made their English premier league football debut, being worn by Portsmouth FC.

Stubbies

'He's my man, but he's one of the boys in his Stubbies . . . Stubbies . . .'
Now there's an advertising jingle to strike fear into the hearts of women
the country over! In the 1970s Kiwi blokes couldn't get enough of their
Stubbies, so much so that they were probably the single most significant
male fashion item of the decade. And guess what? They weren't even
ours — the venerable Stubbie was an import from across the ditch.

In the 1970s there were shorts, there were short shorts, and then
there were Stubbies. They came in multiple shades of brown and blue.
When summer arrived, you'd be likely to see more Stubbies around
a barbecue than mosquitoes and sandflies combined! Yep, they were
quite popular.

The legendary shorts had their origin in 1972, when Philip Levy
and his colleagues at Edward Fletcher & Co realised that there was
room in the Australian clothing market for cheap but rugged men's
shorts. That decided, they set about finding a name for their shorts
over a few beers one evening. As one of them cracked open a stubby
of beer, inspiration hit — and hard! Why not name the shorts after
something most Australian men love already?

The punt paid off. After the first-ever Stubbies television
advertisement aired in Queensland on a Thursday night in July 1972,
a massive 50,000 pairs of Stubbies were sold in Brisbane alone by
Saturday afternoon. By the end of that month 250,000 pairs had
been sold. The Stubbies revolution was well and truly under way. The
brand was so successful for Edward Fletcher & Co that the company
eventually changed its name to Stubbies Clothing Ltd.

Kiwi men can be a little bit shy when it comes to fashion and it took another five years before Stubbies made our shores — we were a year behind the United States, but we were just a bit ahead of Japan and Europe.

By 1980, Stubbies were selling a massive three million pairs of wee shorts a year across all of their markets. But the people behind the shorts weren't going to rest there. They decided to go all fashion on it. Suddenly, Stubbies were available in brown, blue and every pastel hue you can name (and a few you'd probably struggle with!). There were Stubbies with racing stripes and fly fronts. For the traditionalists who'd been wearing them for a while these fancy new pants were a travesty, but they attracted a whole new generation to the short shorts. Total sales of Stubbies reached 300 million pairs.

With the onset of the 90s, Kiwi and Aussie blokes started to get all shy about their legs and the boardshort made a meteoric comeback. Sales of Stubbies fell massively, and eventually New Zealand stopped importing them. But the Stubbies story doesn't end there — they're now owned by the Australian company Pacific Dunlop, which has revived the ailing brand by diversifying a bit and making short AND long shorts. The return of the Stubbies may be just around the corner!

BREAKFAST TIME

Being an inventive bunch, inspiration must often strike Kiwis while they're sitting at the breakfast table reading the paper — after all, each of these products has become a regular breakfast-time feature in homes throughout the country.

Vogel's

One of our favourite sources of breakfast-time fuel is also the source of one of the most often quoted misconceptions about the origin of a New Zealand brand. It's true, we Kiwis love our Vogel's bread . . . so much so that we have a reputation for packing the odd loaf when we go overseas on holiday.

The misunderstanding, surprise surprise, is linked to a politician! The bread is often thought to have been named after Sir Julius Vogel, who was Premier of this country twice in the 1870s. Vogel was born in England to an English mother and a Dutch father. He is not the namesake for the bread.

The Vogel who lives on in our loaves was Dr Alfred Vogel, who was born in Switzerland in 1902, three years after his famous Kiwi namesake died. In his early twenties Vogel took a job in the Swiss city of Basel, managing a healthfood and herb shop. He soon realised the power of plant products in restoring health and establishing a natural harmony in the body. He began creating his own remedies and selling them to customers. Before long he was so well known that he began publishing a health magazine and books on healthy living. Perhaps a man ahead of his time, he summed up his ethos by saying, 'Preventative healthcare is the source of health and happiness. The decision to adopt a well-balanced diet containing natural foodstuffs and to heed the body's own signals must be taken of one's own free will.'

As well as herbal remedies, Vogel was an enthusiastic proponent of using natural whole grains instead of processed wheat. In the 1950s he developed a muesli bread recipe that used whole grains and milk. The recipe gained international attention when it won a gold medal at the Swiss International Food Exhibition.

Dr Vogel's bread recipe made its way to New Zealand in the hands of a man called Johan Klisser. An immigrant from the Netherlands, Klisser started work in 1951 as a baker at the famous Reizenstein's bakery in Auckland's Ponsonby Road. The bakery was a welcome addition to the Auckland foodscape, offering varieties of bread outside the bog standard white and brown. Having learned his trade from Dr Max Reizenstein, Klisser then bought his boss's business and renamed it Klisser's Farmhouse Bakeries.

In the early 1960s the Klissers purchased the franchise rights to produce Dr Vogel's health bread in New Zealand. Before long the bakehouse was baking half a million loaves of Vogel's every week. In 1990 the Klissers sold the bakery and the Vogel's bread recipe to Goodman Fielders, who have continued to build the brand.

And what of Dr Vogel? Well, he visited New Zealand and Australia in 1979 at the age of 77. All that healthy living obviously worked for him as he lived to the ripe old age of 94, dying in the Swiss city of Feusisberg in 1996.

Anathoth

It usually takes a few decades before a brand really establishes itself in the consciousness of the buying public, but not so a brand of jams and relishes that only came into being in the early 1980s. It's only taken about 20 years for the Anathoth brand to become a real favourite on Kiwi breakfast tables. In part its popularity comes from its unusual (and unpronounceable!) name.

Anathoth

Raspberry
Jam

475 g net

Homemade – the way it used to be

72

MADE IN NEW ZEALAND

The Anathoth story started in Upper Moutere, near Nelson, when Owen and Kaye Pope bought a raspberry farm and set up a joinery business. This is where the secret of that strange name comes in. They named the farm Anathoth, pronounced (say after me . . .) arna-tot.

The name has Hebrew origins and is shared with a village north of Jerusalem, which is also called Anata. The village is name-checked several times in the Old Testament, and is best known as the home of the prophet Jeremiah. However, it wasn't because of its long history that the Popes decided to name their farm Anathoth (remember, arna-tot!). It's because in Hebrew the name is thought to mean 'answered prayer', and that's certainly what it was for the Pope family.

In order to promote Owen's new joinery business he and Kaye decided to take a stall at Nelson's famous Saturday market. Kaye had a great idea to make the stall pay for itself — she started making jam from the farm's produce and selling it. Word got round that there was some seriously good homemade jam on offer and the jam would sell out, and fast! Eventually, the joinery business got left behind and it was all hands on deck to produce jam in order to keep up with demand.

The popularity of Nelson's market meant that people from all over the country started talking about this jam they'd bought. After all, everyone loves homestyle jam even if they don't have the time to make it themselves any more. Word got to the ears of the right people at a supermarket chain and they decided to give the Popes a call. From that first raspberry jam recipe, the Anathoth brand grew to include strawberry, apricot, boysenberry and blackberry jams. And jam eaters the country over couldn't get enough of them.

By 1998, the brand was one of the best-selling in the country

Breakfast time

and the company introduced home-style relishes, chutneys and pickles — yet another range of products that our mothers and grandmothers might have made. Recently, Anathoth was bought by another famous Kiwi fruit processor and family firm, Barker's of Geraldine.

Sanitarium

Without Sanitarium, breakfast in New Zealand would be a very different thing indeed. Since the beginning of last century, it's the one company that has dominated our early-day dining. Chances are you've had one of their brands in your pantry recently — Weet-Bix, Ricies, Skippy cornflakes, peanut butter and Marmite — they're all Sanitarium products.

The origins of the company go back to the very origins of breakfast cereals themselves. Like a lot of good stories, this one starts with a dream. On Christmas Day 1865 a woman called Ellen White had a dream that she should establish a health centre that followed the teachings of the Seventh Day Adventist Church, of which she was a member.

White lived in a town called Battle Creek, in Michigan. So it was there that she followed her dream, and the Western Reform Health Clinic opened on 5 September 1866. The centre attracted people with its simple message of natural food and eight hours' sleep a night.

In 1876, a man called John Harvey Kellogg was appointed as medical director of the centre. Recognise that name? Yes, he's the Kellogg of Kellogg's cereals — one of Sanitarium's main competitors! It was Kellogg who changed the name of the clinic to Battle Creek Sanitarium — a sanitarium being what we now know as a sanatorium.

Under the stewardship of Kellogg and his brother the centre became a world-class health spa. They encouraged a natural diet, exercise, fresh air and hygiene.

While running the sanatorium, Kellogg and his brother began to investigate ways to make natural grains, which Kellogg believed were an important part of a healthy diet, more edible. Through their experiments they worked out how to cook wheat and then roll it into flakes. Kellogg then realised that the same process could be carried out with corn kernels.

Before long, the town of Battle Creek became home to a massive 40 cereal manufacturers! But what, apart from the name, does this have to do with Sanitarium? Well, Ellen White, who had first dreamt up the Battle Creek facility, visited the Seventh Day Adventist congregation in Melbourne, Australia. They were impressed with her message and imported some of Kellogg's new-fangled cereal. They then decided to start making their own, and the church set up the Sanitarium company in Melbourne in 1898, the name being a nod to the Battle Creek Sanitarium.

In a bakery in the city, a man called Edward Halsey set about creating Sanitarium's first products. Halsey was a committed Seventh Day Adventist who had trained at Battle Creek under John Kellogg. In Melbourne he created a peanut butter recipe as well as a cereal he called Granose — the forerunner of our Weet-Bix. Soon after, Halsey saw the light and made the move across the Tasman, settling in Christchurch. There he made wholemeal bread and cereal in a wooden shed in Papanui. The food was destined for a health home, but the patients there enjoyed it so much that they wanted to be able to eat it at home.

From that small shed the company has grown and changed,

MADE IN NEW ZEALAND

still under the stewardship of the Seventh Day Adventist church, and keeping true to Kellogg's original beliefs about the link between food and health. It has grown so much that between New Zealand and Australia the company now employs more than 1700 people and makes a range of more than 150 products — all from its beginnings in a Papanui shed!

Chelsea Sugar

When you're drizzling a drop of golden syrup on your morning crumpets or porridge, or sprinkling a bit of sugar on your cereal, have you ever wondered what that building on the packaging is? If you have, chances are you're not an Aucklander. Residents of the Queen city know only too well that it's the Chelsea Sugar Refinery at Birkenhead on the city's North Shore.

The Chelsea Sugar story started in 1882 when the government of the time decided New Zealand needed to stop relying on Australia for sugar production. It offered a fat wad of cash to anyone who would set up a sugar refinery in New Zealand. The Colonial Sugar Refining Company of Australia, the Victorian Sugar Company and a group of very prominent Auckland businessmen, including Messrs Wilson, Horton and Nathan, established the New Zealand Sugar Company in 1883.

The company claimed the government cash and bought 160 acres of land — that's about 65 hectares — on the northern shores of the Waitemata Harbour. Bear in mind there was no harbour bridge at this point, so the North Shore was unconquered farmland, not sprawling suburbs! There were heaps of reasons for choosing the factory's Birkenhead site. It was close to the city, there was abundant flat land for building on, a freshwater creek ran nearby, and the harbour was very deep so big ships would be able to sail right up to the factory's proposed port.

Work building the factory began straight away. Timber was milled from trees on the site and local clay was excavated to make the 1.5 million bricks needed to bring the project to fruition. Machinery was imported from Scotland and raw sugar came from the Pacific Islands, Australia and South America. By 1884 everything was in place, and the refinery began operating around the clock.

The name Chelsea was bestowed on the sugar works, not by some fanatical British football fan, but instead by the refinery's first customs officer — yep, they imported and exported straight from the port, so they had to have their very own government officials. The customs officer was originally from Chelsea in London, and as was the fashion of the day, he decided to bring a little bit of England with him to New Zealand by giving his new home the same name as his old one.

While the sugar industry has been through some ups and downs, the Chelsea refinery has continued operation since it opened in the 1880s. The factory site has expanded to triple its original size, and the company has been responsible for the development of much of the surrounding area. In the 1900s Birkenhead had a population of 1000, with one-third of the male population working at the refinery. The rest of the village relied on the refinery workers for income.

When the harbour bridge was finally built, it had a massive effect on Auckland's development. It's become an icon of the city — but were it not for the Chelsea Sugar Works, the bridge could look very different. One of the main considerations on building the bridge was that ships heading for the refinery had to be able to fit underneath it!

Today, the Chelsea refinery produces an incredible 200,000 tonnes of sugar products each year, and it continues to function around the clock. Many of the buildings in the area are heritage protected, such is their historical importance, and much of the land the refinery sits on is open to the public as parkland.

Bell Tea

Should New Zealand ever become a republic, the Union Jack on the flag might disappear, but there are some British habits Kiwis won't give up so readily. One is *Coronation Street*; another is that great English tradition of tea-drinking.

One of our favourite breakfast-time tipples is Bell Tea. Yes, Bell teabags with that feel-alive flavour . . . Bell teabags for your teacup or your pot. Ring a bell? That jingle has to be one of New Zealand's most enduring pieces of advertising. The Bell brand and its ringing-bell logo have been a fixture in this country since 1898.

Many people think that the Bell name and logo were just a handy symbol for a tea that will wake you up. True, but the real origin of the Bell name comes from one of the company's founders — Norman Harper Bell.

Born in Melbourne, Bell moved to Dunedin in 1894. Not long after he arrived, he began working for R Wilson and Company, a Dunedin grocery company that had been in business since 1862. Bell registered the Bell Tea trademark for the company in 1898 and set about building the Bell Tea name throughout the country. Bell really understood the importance of marketing, and soon introduced competitions and coupons for his product.

By 1905, Norman Harper Bell had left R Wilson & Company and bought the Bell trademark from them. He then established The Bell Tea Company. The years that followed were challenging for the new company. Bell died in 1912, and his son took over as boss of the company. Then along came the First World War. Supplies of tea were sporadic throughout the war but a ruling by the wartime prime minister, William Massey, saw Bell's sales go through the roof.

In order to make it easier for families to send parcels to their boys at the front, the government announced cheaper postage rates for parcels up to a certain size. That size? The exact dimensions of a Bell Tea tin. Families around the country bought up the tea so that they could pack the tins with sweets, cakes, biscuits, socks, gloves — anything that would fit and might cheer up the boys fighting in Europe. The result was that Bell struggled to keep up with demand, and a telltale sign of the presence of New Zealanders at the front was the presence of Bell Tea cans!

After the war, Bell introduced more competitions and coupons to persuade people to keep buying their tea. It worked so well that their opposition complained, and legislation was brought in to regulate the use of these kinds of inducements to buy a product. Bell continued to use what became known as tea coupons, which were like an early precursor of Fly Buys. How it worked was that there would be a wee coupon in the tea packet, which on its own wasn't worth much. You had to keep collecting them up, and when you had enough you sent them to the company who would send you some cash. How much?

Well, in the late 1960s and early 1970s if you saved up 24 coupons you'd get 20 cents; 50 coupons would earn you 55 cents, and 150 coupons would earn you a whopping two dollars. Think about it, that's 150 boxes of tea to earn two bucks (which with inflation and everything would now be worth about $25).

Bell Tea is now New Zealand's most popular tea, despite stiff competition from other tea companies. The Dunedin factory still produces plenty of the amber brew, and the company now has a factory in Auckland as well.

Gregg's coffee

Dunedin can be a tough place for broke students at times. No, not on cold, windy days but rather when the weather's fine and there's no wind. Those are the days when the city is scented with three student staples — chocolate from Cadbury's, beer from Speight's, and coffee from Gregg's. All three products are made in the city and the air is rich with their aromas when the weather's just right.

While Dunedin's links with Speight's and Cadbury's are well-known, Gregg's place in Dunedin is less well-known — except to students who know that the Gregg's plant is almost right on the university campus.

New Zealand's love affair with coffee has been a bit of an inconstant one, but nonetheless the Gregg's brand has survived and grown over the nearly 150 years it's been here. The company was named by its founder William Gregg in 1962. Gregg was the son of an Irish farmer who emigrated to Australia during the gold-rush years.

While he was living in Ballarat in Victoria, Gregg set himself up as a coffee and spice vendor. Like many people, he found that selling stuff to gold miners was an easier way to make money than going out looking for gold himself.

Following the discovery of gold in Otago in 1861, Gregg followed many of his cohorts across the Tasman to try and make a bob or two out of speculators in the new gold rush. He arrived in Dunedin in 1862 and set up business in Moray Place. W Gregg & Co was a general merchant that also happened to roast coffee.

Eventually Gregg moved his premises to the shores of Pelichet Bay — which is now underneath the reclaimed land that includes Logan Park — not far from the company's current premises in Forth St. What success Gregg had was soon all but wiped out by some ill-fated investment in gold dredging, excessive land buying and, most saliently, investing in a chicory farm. The presence of chicory-growing in Gregg's diverse portfolio would not have been unusual for a coffee merchant at the time. While today Kiwis are among the most discerning coffee drinkers in the world, back in the late 1800s things were very different. Coffee roasters often mixed ground beans with chicory.

Luckily for Gregg, he had married well. His wife, Eleanor, was quite wealthy and the company managed to weather the financial difficulties. Gregg died in 1901, and the company remained in the Gregg family until the 1920s when it was bought by a group of shareholders. The company eventually diversified into making a range of products like instant puddings and salad dressings, but coffee has always remained at the core of Gregg's.

In the 1940s, American GIs who came to New Zealand for rest and recreation brought with them a new-fangled product — instant coffee. Their presence saw a resurgence of interest in coffee in New Zealand, but it wasn't until the 1960s that Gregg's introduced their own brand of instant coffee onto the market. This time-saving brew became an instant hit (!) across the country, and it has continued to be a Kiwi favourite ever since.

Creamoata

Throughout the first half of the twentieth century Sergeant Dan was as well-known and popular in this country as Bart Simpson is now. If you don't know who he is, ask your parents or your grandparents (depending on how old you are!) and they're bound to know. Sergeant Dan was a cartoon character who was a big fan of the hearty porridge, Creamoata. In fact, he was even known as Sergeant Dan, the Creamoata Man. Dressed in a military-looking boy scout uniform, Dan encouraged people around the country to eat Creamoata, with catchy ditties like:

I am the man, says Sergeant Dan,
I care not one iota,
For who can be as strong as me,
While I have my Creamoata.

OK, so it's not as catchy as 'Don't have a cow, man', but people back then loved it! Dan's image appeared in advertising, on bowls manufactured to encourage the eating of Creamoata, on envelopes, and a huge picture of him graced the building in Gore where the oats for Creamoata were milled. It's still there today, and even though the mill closed down in 2001 the town is still proud of its mythical military man.

The name Creamoata is a combination of cream and oats, denoting the creamy oat concoction that porridge is advertised to be. Hardly surprising, then, that the man whose company got the whole country eating porridge for breakfast hailed from Scotland. That man was Thomas Fleming.

Born in Lanarkshire in Scotland in 1848, Fleming arrived in Bluff with his family in 1862. Even though he was only 14, Fleming got a job as a gardener in Invercargill. Within two years his father had bought a farm just out of town at Mabel Bush. After working with his father for a few years, Fleming moved north. He got a job harvesting wheat at Totara Estate, just south of Oamaru — the estate has been preserved and you can still go there and see what life would have been like for Fleming.

An ambitious sort of chap, Fleming decided to learn the art of flourmilling, and got a job at a mill at Kakanui. It didn't take long before he was managing the mill, but the lure of the south was strong. In 1875 he moved back to Invercargill to manage a mill there. The following year he and his brother-in-law bought the company. They then set about buying a number of mills around the southern half of the South Island, including one in Gore. The Fleming name has thus been associated with Gore since 1878.

The high population of people of Scottish extraction and the ideal growing conditions for oats on the Southland plains meant it wasn't long before Fleming's decided to start making porridge, which the Fleming's mill in Gore did for more than a hundred years. Though the Creamoata name lives on, it's now produced in Australia by Nestlé, under the Uncle Toby's brand.

Crown Lynn

During the twentieth century there must have been scarcely a family in New Zealand that didn't have a piece of Crown Lynn somewhere in the house — be it a well-used dinner set, a novelty egg-cup, a McAlpine water jug in the fridge, a snaffled Railways cup or one of those legendary swans.

Just as Temuka pottery was developed as a sideline for a company producing ceramic electrical ware, Crown Lynn was born out of a clayworks making bricks and pipes. The company was started in the 1890s in Hobsonville, then merged with a handful of other potteries around the country to form the Amalgamated Brick and Pipe Company in the 1920s. It was around this time that a plant was built in New Lynn that would soon become home to the largest pottery in the southern hemisphere (and by pottery I mean a place that produces pots, not a really huge ashtray!).

Amalgamated Brick and Pipe Co (Ambrico for short) might have carried on making pipes and bricks until it went out of business had it not been for the grandson of the company's founder. Tom Clark went into the family business at the age of 14 and quickly learned all there was to know about making bricks and pipes. He could also see that if the company didn't diversify it wouldn't survive another slump like the one it went through during the Depression of the twenties. Over the next 20 years the company made tiles and porcelain components for electrical ware. They even made some crockery for the US Army during the Second World War.

Then came the famous Railways cup. Because of the war, New Zealand couldn't import English crockery so Ambrico and Temuka

Pottery set about making the dangerously weighty cups that have become a Kiwiana icon. The cups were so heavy that one wag reckoned that if there was a nuclear war only ants, cockroaches and New Zealand Railways cups would survive! The first of the cups made in Auckland were produced under the Ambrico name, as Crown Lynn didn't come about until 1948.

While the company had already started making the crockery and decorative ware for which it became famous, Tom Clark decided that it needed a new name. This was partly because the company was having a bit of a tough time financially, due to a rapidly changing postwar market and the high value of the New Zealand dollar making exports less viable (sound familiar?).

Given that the company had moved on so far from the bricks and pipes of its early days, Clark reckoned the new name needed to reflect the business as it stood. Crown Lynn was decided on as it had an air of quality about it. It also harked back to the British potteries, many of whose names were preceded by Crown — think Crown Devon, Royal Crown Derby, Crown Staffordshire . . . The other thing these names have in common is that the Crown is followed by the place they're made in. Thus Crown Lynn was born. Among the first products to bear the new name were the now-famous Crown Lynn swans.

At the height of business in the 1970s Crown Lynn employed about 500 people and turned out some 15 million pieces of china every year. But the boom wasn't to last. With deregulation of the New Zealand economy in the 1980s the market was flooded with cheap imported ceramics and Crown Lynn just couldn't compete. Its factory closed in 1989 and in 1993 a Malaysian company bought the brand. It continues to produce under the Crown Lynn name in Kuala Lumpur today.

AROUND THE
HOUSE

5

Look around your place — how much of the
stuff in it was invented in New Zealand? You
might just be surprised . . .

Tux dog biscuits

There are more than half a million dogs in this country — that's a lot of mouths to feed. Up until the 1950s they were pretty much all fed meat of varying quality and nutritional value. Some dogs were treated pretty well but there were lots that weren't, which got a Blenheim man thinking.

Tiny Moore reckoned he could come up with a dog food that would be nutritious, easy to store and quick to feed. Possibly inspired by a bit of home baking, he got the idea of mixing up a batch of meaty biscuits for feeding to our canine companions. Tiny tried out a few different recipes and finally hit upon one that he reckoned the dogs would love. The only problem now was finding a company to make them for him.

He went to see the blokes at a Blenheim company called Elastrator. Yep, they produced exactly what their name suggests — those little elastic bands farmers use to castrate lambs. They were also very clued in to what farmers would be likely to pay money for.

Tiny had a good trick up his sleeve while he was meeting the Elastrator man. He took a big, juicy steak with him, as well as some of his large, hard, baked dog biscuits. He covered each of these with a sack and waited for the dogs to come sniffing around. It could all have gone horribly wrong, but the dogs were impressed with Tiny's canine culinary ability and went straight for the sack that was covering the plate of his dog biscuits. Elastrator was on board and Tiny Moore had found himself a biscuit manufacturer!

The name for these doggy delights? Tux. The word Tux is not derived from a tuxedo (that'd be pretty daft when you're trying to sell the product to farmers more comfortable in Swanndris than suits). Instead Tux is a shortened form of dog tucker, meaning dog food. The first commercially made Tux dog biscuits were produced in a Blenheim bakehouse in 1954. The product proved to be so popular with farmers that a purpose-built factory was opened in Blenheim in 1959. Tux production was moved from Blenheim to Marton in 1967 to make the most of the wheat and milk being produced in the Marton area. Tux continues to be made there today.

Tux's popularity was based on a number of factors. First and foremost the dogs liked eating them. The farmers liked buying them because they gave their dogs a balanced and nutritional diet without too much fuss. But Tux also brought important health benefits.

Hydatids, a lethal disease for dogs that is carried by a tapeworm, was prevalent in New Zealand at the time. Dogs could pick up the tapeworm from raw meat or offal. In order to try and prevent the spread of this disease, the government outlawed the feeding of raw meat or offal to working dogs. Farmers had to look for another source of food for their dogs and Tux was the obvious replacement. Sales boomed, and the move to ban feeding raw meat was so successful that the country has recently been declared hydatids-free — making it one of the few places in the world that has managed to eliminate the disease.

Masport lawnmowers

Any given weekend in this country, there's hardly a suburb that doesn't buzz with the sound of lawns being mowed (except when it's raining, of course!). Kiwis love their gardens, and one of the most important parts of a well-kept garden is a regularly manicured lawn. While some of us just mow the lawn when it gets a bit long, there are other New Zealanders who take an inordinate amount of pride in having an even, symmetrical lawn of a consistent length. Whether your thing is a cut or a coif, there's one Kiwi company whose machinery has probably trimmed your lawn. That firm is Masport.

In 2010, it will be one hundred years since the company's two founders first joined forces. Back in 1910, Harold Mason and Rueben Porter decided to set up their own engineering business. At that stage the company was called Mason and Porter Ltd, but they later combined the Mas from Mason and the Port from Porter to become Masport. They took premises on Auckland's Greys Ave and began to manufacture vacuum pumps and engines to power farm equipment. (It's hard to imagine today's residents of Greys Avenue being too thrilled about such heavy manufacturing going on in the middle of the city!)

For the next 20 years Mason and Porter Ltd continued working with the agricultural sector and developing new products for farmers. But New Zealand was becoming more urbanised, and people were moving to big sections in the suburbs. A side effect of this was that city folk were becoming less and less keen on keeping a goat or a sheep in the backyard to keep the lawns down! So in 1930 Mason and Porter decided to diversify slightly. They built their first lawnmower.

It was a hand-powered mower that you had to push (that's right, a lawnmower that didn't have a motor or — if you're really flash — a seat to sit on as you drove it around!). The mower was called the Cleveland, named after Cleveland Road in Parnell, where the company was then based.

The Cleveland had five blades that would turn as you pushed it and a roller that would flatten the grass after it was cut. You could adjust the height of the blades depending on how short you wanted the grass and, if you were really flash, you could get a pimped-out version that had rubber tyres so your lawnmower didn't make too much noise as you wheeled it across concrete paths!

The amazing thing about these Cleveland push-mowers is that you still see people using them today. They were incredibly sturdy, built from hardened steel, and they just needed a bit of oil and the odd blade sharpen to keep them going. For those of you who can't imagine using a push-mower, never fear. In 1938 Masport introduced the country's first petrol-powered lawnmower, and Lawnsprites (to appeal to the ladies) and Lawnchiefs (for the blokes out there!) became the mowers of choice. Such was the popularity of the Masport motor-mowers — and the upper arm workout you got from trying to start them — the company had to move to bigger premises, so in 1938 they moved to their current site in Auckland's Mt Wellington.

Like many other companies, the Second World War had a huge impact on Masport. Instead of building lawnmowers, the company started to produce things like gun carriers to help with the war effort. After the war, Kiwis went back to mowing their lawns and Masport continued to make lawnmowers. Soon the Australians realised how good our lawns were looking and Masport started to export mowers across the Tasman, where they now have about 15 per cent of the lawnmower market.

From its small start in central Auckland, Masport has grown to employ nearly 200 people, making a whole range of outdoor products for both the New Zealand market and about 35 other countries, including the Netherlands, Belgium and China. While they're now also renowned for making patio heaters, barbecues and other garden implements like chippers and splitters, the company is still best known for that one product it was built on — bloody good lawnmowers!

Yates

When Arthur Yates climbed aboard a ship to New Zealand in the 1870s he couldn't possibly have imagined that he was sailing towards setting up a business that would become one of the biggest garden supply companies in New Zealand and Australia, let alone that he would write a book that would eventually sell more than eight million copies!

It wasn't even the opportunities afforded to those emigrating to New Zealand that drew Arthur Yates to this country. It was his health. Arthur was born in the north of England in 1861, and from the age of 15 he had worked in the family's seed business in Manchester. At that time Manchester was one of Europe's industrial powerhouses, and with industry came pollution. Arthur Yates suffered from chronic asthma and at the age of 28 he decided that, for the sake of his health, he'd head for the clear air of New Zealand.

Yates arrived on the *Auckland* on 23 December 1879. He spent a

The "Boys" will be coming home sooner than some people expect. . . . Most of our sacrifices have been nothing to theirs.. . . . You should at least make a better garden before they return, because gardening is a war-time duty. NOW is the time to make a start!

1943

YATES' AUTUMN GARDEN CALENDAR

couple of years working on farms in Otago, and while working on the land he realised that there was a need for good quality seeds. So in 1883 he moved to Auckland and opened a small seed shop in Victoria St. Not satisfied with being a shopkeeper, Yates travelled the country to spread the word about his new business and take orders from farmers as he went.

In 1886 he went to Sydney, and while there he realised that the Australians could do with some good seed stock too, so he employed a salesman there to take orders for seeds. A year later, Arthur's brother Ernest arrived in New Zealand and joined the business. Still suffering from his asthma and knowing the company would be in good hands in New Zealand, Arthur moved to Sydney where the climate was more forgiving.

Until 1893 the company had largely just supplied agricultural clients, but the Yates realised that home gardeners could benefit from their expertise. They started to sell small packets of seeds to gardeners, branding them Yates Reliable Seeds. The popularity of the seeds for the home market led Arthur Yates to start writing a book to answer the questions he was asked most often by customers. The *Yates' Gardening Guide for Australia and New Zealand: Hints for Amateurs* was first published in 1895. It was such a success that Yates updated it every year, adding information on new seeds and plants as well as new plant-management techniques.

Since its first publication, 76 editions of the *Yates Garden Guide* have been produced, and more than seven million copies sold — it is undoubtedly one of New Zealand's bestselling books ever and an indispensible part of most Kiwi gardeners' arsenals.

In the meantime the seed business continued to grow on both

sides of the Tasman. In 1906 the Yates brothers decided to split the two operations, and they were to remain separate until the Australian company bought out its Kiwi counterpart in the 1980s.

Arthur Yates passed away in 1926, but the Yates family continued to run the company until 1951 when it became a shareholder-owned company. On this side of the ditch the company continued to grow, with branches opening around the country and products diversifying from seeds to fertilisers, tools, potting mixes — think of just about any product you'd use in the garden and Yates probably make it.

Resene Paints

It's amazing what desperation and a concrete mixer can cause a can-do Kiwi to do. In Ted Nightingale's case, the combo saw him establish one of New Zealand's most successful and innovative paint companies.

In 1946, Nightingale was working as a builder and living in the picturesque town of Eastbourne, on the eastern shores of Wellington harbour. With the Second World War over, there was plenty of demand for skilled builders and Ted was putting up a lot of buildings using concrete. The only problem was that he needed a paint that would be alkali-resistant, thereby preventing chemical reactions that can cause concrete to crack. There was nothing like this on the market so Ted did what any self-respecting Kiwi bloke of the time would do — he headed for his garage. Out there, he experimented with a few combinations and finally hit upon a paint recipe that would do exactly what he needed it to do.

Word soon got out that Nightingale had sussed out a product

that was perfect for painting concrete, and other painters and builders came flocking. Ted realised that he had something of a hit on his hands, and he started to produce his magic paint on a commercial basis under the name Stipplecote. Realising that he had a bit of a knack for this paint lark, but that the garage was getting a bit full, Ted Nightingale set up his Stipplecote Products' first paint factory in Wellington's Tinakori Rd.

Not content with bringing alkali-resistant paint to New Zealand, Nightingale set about developing a water-based paint that could be used outdoors. One of the key ingredients of the paint was resin, so what else to call that paint but Resene. In 1951 Resene paints were launched around the country, but people were a bit suspicious of the company's claims that the paint would stick to your house but not to your brushes. In order to counter this, the company undertook a massive marketing campaign. In shop windows and hardware stores around the country, people would look on amazed when Resene salespeople would paint boards and then rinse their brushes in water!

Eventually this new-fangled idea caught on and people stopped using unhealthy lead-based paints in favour of Resene's waterborne product. The company got so busy that they had to move to a factory in Kaiwharawhara. They stayed there a few years before moving to another new factory in Lower Hutt's Seaview in 1967.

In 1972, the second generation of Nightingales, Ted's son Tony, took over the helm of the company. It was Tony who decided to take Resene in a new direction. Instead of relying on other people to sell its paint, the company employed its own salespeople throughout the country. The success of this, and its purchase of a wallpaper company, saw Resene's first foray into direct retail sales to the public.

The establishment of the Resene paint shops almost happened by happy coincidence in 1975. The wallpaper firm the company had bought had a shop in Marion St, in central Wellington. Resene decided to keep the shop and open the somewhat obviously named Marion St Paint Shop! The shop was staggeringly successful and led to the opening of ColorShops in Auckland, Hamilton, Hawke's Bay, Christchurch and Dunedin before the end of the year.

Two years later, the reputation of Resene paint was such that the company name was changed from Stipplecote Products Ltd to Resene Paints Ltd. With continuing success came a new factory in Naenae in 1992, and in 1999 the third generation of Nightingales, Tony's son Nick, became general manager of the company.

While it's still a family company, the paint production that began in Ted Nightingale's Eastbourne garage has become an industry that employs over 500 staff, with 55 ColorShops throughout the country.

Para Pools

When George Skjellerup opened the first Para Rubber store in Christchurch in 1910 the company was focused on making stuff like milking-machine parts and tyres. Their motto was 'We have it in stock, will get it, or it isn't made of rubber'. The whole rubber thing even extended to the company's name — Para being a region of Brazil that produced a lot of the sticky stuff.

While the company became pretty famous for their hot-water bottles, raincoats and other handy stuff, it was really the advent of the Para Pool that saw the company's name become part of everyday Kiwi

language. Para Pools eventually became so popular that any above-ground backyard pool in this country ended up becoming known as a Para Pool even if it wasn't one.

The pools were invented in the United States in the 1950s when a company called Doughboy worked out that if you glued a PVC sheet to a metal frame you could make a cheap and portable pool. A chap called Doug Clark started importing the Doughboy pools into Australia, and before long he had started building similar pools for the Aussie market. Clark improved on the American model by developing a low-cost filtering system for the pool. Sales took off and Australian backyards the country over became home to Clark pools.

What does this have to do with us? Well, Doug Clark was mates with Doug Davies, who just happened to be the managing director of a wee Kiwi company called Para Rubber. The two Dougs got their heads together and decided to see how these new-fangled pools would go on this side of the Tasman. They tested the market here with a few smaller pools, which sold well, encouraging Para to invest further in the development of local products.

Para expanded the range of pools available and set about teaching their store staff how the pools, and all their accompanying pumps, filters and bits, worked. One way of encouraging the store managers to push the pools in their shops was to give them an up-close look at a pool during one of their conferences. Disaster struck! The fastening system on the demo pool hadn't been put together properly and it burst — the attendant wave knocking MD Doug Davies to the ground! This inauspicious start, combined with the cost of setting up the pool side of the business, led company chairman Valdemar Skjellerup to say repeatedly that he thought the pools

MADE IN NEW ZEALAND

would bankrupt the company. For once, the boss got it wrong.

The pool side of Para's business absolutely took off. Kiwis have always loved the water, and more of them saw the benefit of a pool in the backyard with every passing summer. By 1975 Para Pool sales peaked at 10,000 for the year. The company still make and sell pools, and with the skyrocketing cost of coastal real estate their catchphrase 'better than a beach in your own backyard' has never been more true!

Fisher & Paykel

Think about an average meal in your house. Chances are it goes something like this: grab some food out of the fridge, cook it in the oven, serve it, spill something on the tablecloth, finish your dinner, clear the table, stack the dishwasher, chuck the grubby tablecloth in the washing machine, freeze the leftovers. Sound familiar? It's a ritual Kiwi families go through all the time, and chances are that either the fridge, oven, dishwasher, washing machine or freezer were made by Fisher and Paykel.

Despite the company's recent move to do all their manufacturing offshore, the Fisher and Paykel story is a very New Zealand one. Two young entrepreneurs, Woolf Fisher and Maurice Paykel, got together to form the company in 1934. Their first business venture was selling fridges that had been imported by Paykel's family business. They opened a retail shop in Queen's Arcade on Auckland's Queen St and gradually expanded their range to include vacuum cleaners, toasters and other small household electrical goods.

By 1938 the store was going pretty well but the pair were

struggling to get hold of stock due to government import restrictions. There was only one thing for it — they were going to have to start manufacturing their own stock. Initially they did this under licence for other companies (such as Kelvinator), then while the company was still getting on its feet as a manufacturer the Second World War started. The government declared the manufacturing of washing machines and fridges to be an essential industry. This gave Fisher & Paykel an unexpected boost — they managed to keep all their staff on, and continued to fill increasing orders throughout the war. The business was going so well that they had to move to a new factory.

They weren't there long, though, before they moved to a purpose-built plant in Auckland's Mt Wellington in 1956. It was at this factory that the first products bearing the Fisher & Paykel name were produced. Fisher & Paykel had invested plenty of money in the design of their own appliances, nurturing engineers and encouraging their experimentation. The first appliance of their own design, a pressurised clothes dryer, rolled off the production line in 1956. The following year a Fisher & Paykel-designed dual fridge-freezer went into production.

This tradition of innovation and experimentation has become a key part of Fisher & Paykel's company ethos. Their biggest splash of recent years was their revolutionary new dishwasher, the DishDrawer. Until its release, dishwashers were pretty much one-size-fits-all. But two men working for the company, engineer Adrian Sargeant and designer Phil Brace, reckoned they could switch the old-style dishwasher up a wee bit. Basing their design on a filing cabinet, they created a dishwasher with two independent drawers — a seemingly simple change that has revolutionised the dishwasher market.

Tullen Snips

Remember back when you were at school and you weren't allowed to have a proper pair of scissors in case you ran with them and accidentally stabbed one of your classmates? Craft corner was made much more challenging through the lack of scissors — that is, until a couple of Kiwis came up with an invention that was blunt enough to be safe for kids but could also cut paper and other materials. They were called Tullen Snips, and by the late 1970s they were in nearly every classroom and heaps of homes around the country.

The Tullen Snips story started when John Hough and Newman Locke got hold of a pair of Argentinean garden shears in 1972. The secret behind the shears was that they were made out of heat-treated steel — this made the steel incredibly hard, and able to take on the toughest of materials. Hough and Locke decided that they would try to replicate the technology in a Kiwi design. They set about heat-treating some steel but the process was a bit hit and miss to start with — the biggest miss resulting in them having to hiff out 20,000 pairs of shears . . . so it was back to the drawing board.

Eventually they came up with a process that was even better than the original heat-treating they'd been trying to perfect. The new method meant that they could punch the shears out of sheet steel and then heat-treat them. Unlike other such shears, these new ones never needed to be sharpened. They also had a blunt cutting edge that made them ideal for use around the house and garden, and meant that they were much safer for kids to use. The men dubbed their product Tullen Snips. The initial product was probably more at home in the garden than anywhere else in the house, but soon a specifically

designed kitchen version was on the market.

Another innovation that came with the Kitchen Cutters was their unique wall-holder. You'd hang the holder somewhere handy in the kitchen and be able to just grab the Cutters whenever you needed them — no fossicking around in the third drawer down trying to find something to cut that bit of string you're trussing the chook with!

The success of the Kitchen Cutters led to the company working with the Ministry of Education to develop a similar product to be used in Kiwi schools. This saw the introduction of another product in the Snips range — Mini Snips. These were a smaller version of the standard Snips that were ideal for smaller hands. They were so safe that they ended up in schools throughout the country — a real bonus for the art of collaging the country over!

As well as selling strongly in this country, the product was a hit overseas as well. By 1976, Tullen had sold 8 million pairs of Snips in 28 countries around the globe. One of the biggest orders was for 3.25 million pairs, from an Italian dishwashing-detergent manufacturer who included them with packets of their product in order to boost sales.

Business was booming by the time British company Wilkinson Sword bought the company out in 1985. They kept manufacturing the Snips for a while at the company's Auckland plant, but eventually manufacturing stopped and Tullen Snips were assigned to the history books. They were so good though, that there are plenty of Kiwi houses that still have them hanging on the kitchen wall.

Fairydown

The night before Tenzing Norgay and Edmund Hillary's legendary summiting of Mt Everest, they slept in New Zealand-made Fairydown sleeping bags. Hillary wrote later to the manufacturers, 'I don't think there's much doubt that your bags are the best that can be obtained anywhere in the world'. High praise indeed — and words that put the company in the international spotlight.

The Fairydown brand might never have come into being, let alone gone up Everest, had events on 1 January 1874 gone slightly differently. Ephraim and Christina Ellis and their family were on board the immigrant ship *Surat*, on the last leg of their journey from Yorkshire to Port Chalmers, when the ship struck a reef and started to take on water. The passengers saw the steamer *Wanganui* come into view and thought it would be their saviour, but it was not to be. The captain of the *Surat* was drunk and threatened to shoot his passengers if they let on there was a problem! Luckily for the 271 passengers, the ship beached just north of the Catlins River mouth and they escaped with no loss of life.

Some weeks later the Ellis family arrived in Dunedin with little more than the clothes they stood up in. Arthur Ellis's parents soon went to work at the Kaikorai Valley woollen mill but a couple of years later Ephraim Ellis set up his own business producing flock for local upholsterers. It wasn't the most lucrative of businesses, and Arthur joined his father at the age of 13 in 1882. Before long he persuaded his father that they should be importing kapok to replace the flock, and by 1901 the company was manufacturing mattresses.

In 1911 Arthur bought his father's share of the company, and

Arthur Ellis Ltd was born. By the 1920s Arthur's sons were gradually taking over the running of the company. One of them, Roland, was a keen outdoorsman and in 1927 he became one of the few people ever to have climbed Mt Aspiring, near Wanaka. On that ascent, the climbers carted heavy woollen blankets to the top of the mountain. Frustrated by the weight of the blankets, Roland Ellis hit upon an idea. Why not make a fabric bag and stuff it with down. It'd be nice and warm, and very light.

The following year, Roland Ellis made the very first Fairydown sleeping bag — it was a cotton sateen bag stuffed with duck feathers.

MADE IN NEW ZEALAND

The company continued to manufacture mattresses, but they added down quilts and sleeping bags to their product range. The earliest sleeping bags were mostly sold to climbers and trampers, and were very much a supplementary product to other bedding ranges.

That all changed in 1953. Once Edmund Hillary's glowing endorsement of his Fairydown sleeping bag was made public, orders came flooding in. Production almost tripled, from 2000 in 1953 to 5500 in 1955. The popularity of their sleeping bag led the way to developing other outdoor gear including tents, backpacks and ski clothing — with a range of waterproof parkas becoming a mysterious fashion hit in the mid-1980s.

In 1989 the Ellis family's involvement with the company ended when it was sold to a Danish company, Northern Feather. The Fairydown brand then went through a succession of owners and gradually faded from the scene — that was until it was bought recently by Campbell Junor, Bernard Wicht and Pierre van Noorden, who have all worked in other companies producing outdoor gear. They plan to restore the brand to its place as a market leader, so watch this space . . .

6

The first person to brew beer in this country was Captain James Cook, who whipped up a brew when visiting Dusky Sound. It would be fair to say that Kiwis are fond of a drink, so much so that we've come up with quite a few of our own.

Speight's

There's a story often told around Southland (but hardly ever in Otago) that the name Speight's stands for Superb P*ss Enjoyed In Great Hotels Throughout Southland. The reason Otago folk won't tell that story? Because they know the truth, and the truth is that Speight's is named after one of the brewery's founders, James Speight.

The favourite brew of southern men (and women) came into existence way back in 1876, possibly as a result of the university in Dunedin being opened in 1869! The famous amber brew was the brainchild of businessman James Speight, maltster Charles Greenslade and brewer William Dawson. The trio met while working together at Well Park Brewery in north Dunedin, which later became the city's famous whisky distillers, Wilson's.

They set to work quickly and the very first brew of Speight's was produced on 4 April of the same year. The company's founding trio must have liked it because the next day they signed the official documents establishing James Speight and Company. Speight knew the power of marketing, and the very first Speight's advertisement appeared on 23 June in the *New Zealand Tablet*, the national magazine of the Catholic church, which was published in Dunedin.

In 1876 the company also bought the Well Park Brewery's bottling plant in Rattray St, on the same site where Speight's still stands today — back then it was called the City Brewery. Before long the company's beers were winning awards in international competitions and business was so good they built a new brewhouse.

One of the great things about the company's Rattray St site was that there was a freshwater spring running beneath it. Given that

MADE IN NEW ZEALAND

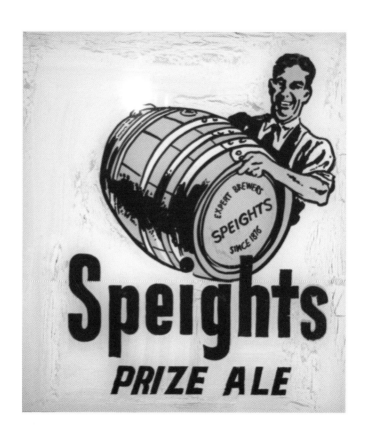

Liquid refreshment

Dunedin's tap water is pretty ordinary now, it must have been even worse back then, so Speight's started to be made with water from the spring.

James Speight died in 1887 at the age of 53 and, unusually for the time, his wife Mary Ann took over his role in managing the company — possibly becoming the first true southern woman!

Speight's managed to survive the threat of prohibition, and by 1917 Charles, Mary Ann and James's son, had become managing director. It was during his reign that Speight's first started being 'exported' to Auckland, with weekly consignments being sent on what became known as the 'Mercy Ship'.

In 1923 Speight's amalgamated with nine smaller companies to form New Zealand Breweries, a move that later almost proved fatal for the famous brew. In 1960 New Zealand Breweries launched a national beer brand ironically called 'Lucky'. As a result of this, Speight's and a number of other regional brands were taken off the market. It's almost enough to bring tears to the eyes of a southerner. Thankfully, the shock of the decision wore off quickly and the southern drinking public made their displeasure known — Speight's was back on the market by the end of the year.

The company's southern heritage was underscored in 1982 when it ran a competition to find a new slogan. The winner of the contest came up with 'Follow the stars' — ring any bells? Probably not, because the runner-up, 'Pride of the South', is the slogan that now emblazons the company's fine product!

Possibly one of the company's finest moments came on April Fool's Day 1998 — almost 122 years to the day since the first Speight's was brewed. The company, in cahoots with the *Otago Daily Times*,

published a story saying that the spring-water tap outside the brewery was pouring a new brew called 'In the Dark' ale. Such is the passion for the amber nectar in Dunedin that quite a crowd gathered, baffled as to why their riggers were still being filled with water!

Hansells

Back in the days before bottled water, sports water, sports drinks and cheap fizzy, kids used to get home after school and tuck into great big glasses of cordial — much of it made by one company, Hansells.

Long before Jungle Juice, Quench and Thriftee had been thought of, Lionel 'LB' Maunsell recognised a gap in the New Zealand food market for good quality locally made food flavourings and essences. The idea was all good, but the execution was a little trickier. That was until he crossed paths with an industrial chemist by the name of Dr Hansen.

The pair joined forces and names in 1934 with the establishment of Hansells Laboratories, setting up in a converted chicken factory in Masterton, where the Hansells factory — much changed — remains today.

Among their early products were food essences that were a combination of flavoured oil, alcohol and water — otherwise known as an emulsion. Rather than being a drawback, Maunsell realised that there was benefit to be had from the cloudy appearance of his products, and he marketed them as 'cloudy for strength'. Two of their top-selling flavours were peppermint and vanilla, both of which were regularly used in home baking.

This was just one of LB Maunsell's excellent marketing ideas. He also did a very smart thing in forging an alliance with Aunt Daisy, the country's first celebrity cook. Her radio show on the ZB network was one of the most popular in the country. If Hansells products were good enough for Aunt Daisy, then they were good enough for her listeners, and sales took off.

In 1945 the company dropped the Laboratories from their name, becoming just Hansells. Around the same time LB retired from the company, leaving it in the safe hands of his son John.

It was not until 1963 that Hansells produced the first of their trio of cordials. That was the year that Quench first came on to the market. It came in liquid form and lurid colours, and you had to dilute it with water before drinking it.

While Quench was pretty popular it was Jungle Juice that really caught the imagination of a generation. It was a powdered drink that came in sachets. You mixed it with a cup of sugar and half a gallon of water, which was handy as that was the amount of water (or beer) that fitted in a beer flagon (otherwise known as a peter if you're from certain parts of the South Island).

Before it was released, Hansells was a bit worried about the name Jungle Juice as the term had been quite commonly used to describe sly grog made by servicemen in the Pacific during the Second World War. Any confusion was shortlived when the teetotal version of Jungle Juice hit the shelves. The product was marketed by a larger-than-life crowd of jungle animals, with the lion and tiger leading the way.

Following the launch of Jungle Juice, the Hansells brains went back to liquid concentrates and released the Thriftee line, which was really just a sugar-free version of Quench designed for the diabetic market.

Jungle Juice disappeared from shelves for a while but has recently made a return as, you guessed it, a liquid concentrate, so it's almost as if Hansells combined the best bits of their trio of drinks and built one super-product!

Tui beer

Tui was thought up by Aucklanders as a way of getting the rest of the country to drink their beer. Yeah, right!

Long before the billboard campaign that brought the Tui Brewery's East India Pale Ale to the attention of the rest of the country, the citizens of Wairarapa and Hawke's Bay were quietly enjoying their local beer.

The Tui story has been inextricably linked with the town of Mangatainoka in northern Wairarapa, between Pahiatua and Woodville, ever since Henry Wagstaff first arrived there in 1889. Wagstaff, who may have lived up to the wag part of his name, later told people that he'd stopped to brew a cup of tea next to the Mangatainoka River early in 1889. That brew, he declared, was the best he'd ever had, and he put its quality down to the water in the river. He'd already been thinking about setting up a brewery and he decided that this would be the perfect spot for it.

Within months, Wagstaff had bought the land next to the river and set about building a brewery there. While his dream was to 'export quality brews to beer drinkers around the colony', Wagstaff had to be

content with conquering the region, before selling the brewery to one Mr Isherwood in 1896. Isherwood's reign was a brief one, and in 1903 he sold the business and Wagstaff's recipes to Henry Cowan.

Like Wagstaff, Cowan had some pretty lofty plans for the place. With national dominance in mind, he renamed it the North Island Brewing Company. Within a year, Tui East India Pale Ale had won a prize at the Palmerston North A&P Show. Word got out that Cowan's beer was just as good as Wagstaff's, and sales continued to grow.

Cowan renamed the brewery after his best-selling beer in 1923 and so the Tui Brewery came into being. Eight years later, the iconic seven-storey brick brewing tower was built — although rumour has it that the builders (who may or may not have been a little distracted by the company's fine product) didn't build any stairs or a lift inside it, so it didn't come into use until 1938. The building is now heritage listed and you won't have to wait outside long before you see a carload of young people pull up to pay homage to the home of their favourite drop!

In 1969 DB Breweries bought Tui and modernised the plant, but it was a few years yet before the rest of the country was allowed in on the secret of Tui. In the 1990s Massey and Victoria university students started to spread the word about Tui, as did shearing gangs heading to the South Island for seasonal work. This word of mouth was backed up by Tui's legendary 'Yeah, right' billboard campaign, which is tailored to various parts of the country — so you'll never see billboards saying 'Wintry blast hits Auckland — Yeah, right' in Auckland, but you might just see it in Winton!

Mac's

If you had to try and think of a quintessentially Kiwi tale of entrepreneurship then it would probably go something like this: rugby-playing garbage collector plays representative rugby, becomes an All Black, then opens a boutique brewery that brews some of the country's favourite beer.

Sounds like a tall tale, doesn't it? Well, it might but it's a true story. It's the story of Terry McCashin and Mac's beer.

Originally from Levin, McCashin was first selected for his province, Horowhenua, in 1963. He then moved to Wellington where he, like quite a few other players at the time, got a job on a garbage truck as it was one of the few jobs where you got paid and kept fit as well. McCashin made the Wellington team in 1967 and the following year he was picked for the All Black squad, where he was a reserve hooker for three seasons. On his retirement from the sport in 1977, McCashin had played 93 first-class games over 15 seasons.

The lure of life in Nelson drew Terry McCashin across Cook Strait. While travelling in England, he had seen the popularity of boutique breweries. He reckoned the same thing could work well here. Back in Nelson, he saw that the Rochdale Cider factory in Stoke was vacant. It was the ideal spot in which to set up a small-scale brewery. McCashin inherited not just the factory but the leftover unused cider bottles, which he used for his first brews — hence the origin of Mac's unusual-shaped ridged bottles!

In 1981, McCashin's Brewery was opened by none other than the prime minister of the day, Sir Robert Muldoon, who described the brewery as a 'David' in an industry of 'Goliaths'. One of the things that really set the brewery apart from the Goliaths was that the beers it brewed conformed to one of the earliest rules of brewing — the Bavarian Purity Laws of 1516. These laws said that only malt, yeast, hops and water could be used to make beer. Mac's lack of chemicals, preservatives and flavourings meant the beer tasted bloody good — and customers just kept coming back.

Mac's beer was so popular that it was named the Best Small Brewery in Australasia in the early 1990s. Then in 1999 a weird twist on Rob Muldoon's David and Goliath analogy occurred. One of the Goliaths, Lion Breweries, adopted the David. Terry McCashin retained ownership of the Nelson brewery but Lion bought the Mac's brand, continuing to brew it in Nelson as well as in Auckland. Fortunately, despite the sale of the brand, Lion has remained true to Terry McCashin's vision of producing quality natural beers.

Corbans

The wine industry in this country is often thought of as relatively new, with our Marlborough sauvignon blancs and Central Otago pinot noirs drawing attention overseas. The truth of the matter is that the craft of the winemaker has been practised here since the late nineteenth century.

One name that is linked with the development of a wine industry in this country is that of the Corban family. They were pioneers in New Zealand wine, establishing a vineyard in Henderson in West Auckland in 1902.

The Corban wine story started in 1864 when Assid Abraham

New Zealand

120
MADE IN NEW ZEALAND

Corban (AA for short) was born in Lebanon. Corban worked in his family's stonemasonry business in Lebanon, but he also worked in the family's vineyard. Unrest in the country and an uncertain economy led AA Corban to leave Lebanon for the South Pacific in 1891, leaving behind his wife and their two children. After spending some time in Victoria, Australia, he arrived in Auckland in 1892.

Originally Corban worked as a travelling salesman before setting up a shop in Queen St selling fancy stuff like jewellery, cosmetics and fabrics. By 1898 things were looking pretty good for AA Corban and he sent for his family. They were soon reunited after a break of seven years, and over the next wee while their family of four turned into a family of 12, with another eight children being born after Najibie Corban joined her husband in New Zealand.

At first the family lived above the shop in Queen St, but AA wanted a better life for them. When the opportunity arose in 1902 to buy four hectares of land in Henderson he grabbed it. Some people thought Corban was a little mad to pay £320 for the land (the equivalent of about $50,000 today), but he knew what he was doing. The soil was right, there was a stream running nearby and the railway was within a stone's throw. This was perfect land for the vineyard he named Mt Lebanon after his homeland.

Vines were planted almost straight away and within a few years Corban was producing the first of the wines he was to become so famous for. Within ten years the vineyard had trebled in size, reflecting the increasing reputation of the Corban name. And this despite the fact that Henderson was in the throes of prohibition. Luckily for the Corbans, legislation was passed allowing winemakers within the prohibition area to continue producing wine. They were

lucky too that the border of the dry area was the railway track outside their house, so they just rented a cottage over the road to sell their product from!

At the 1913–14 Auckland Exhibition the Corbans won a gold medal each for their port and sherry, and their cabernet and riesling each won silver in the competition, which featured wines from throughout the Empire.

The company continued to grow and thrive, and when AA Corban passed away in 1941 it was the biggest wine producer in the country. The business remained in the family, and five of AA's sons converted it into a company in 1963, selling a limited shareholding to liquor wholesalers around the country as a means to increase sales. The family continued to run the company until 1978 when Rothman Industries took control. Even though the Corban family no longer owns their eponymous company, the Corban name and the legacy of the family's patriarch will be linked to the wine industry in this country for many years to come.

Steinlager

While Dunedin has Speight's, Nelson has Mac's and Greymouth has Monteith's, Auckland doesn't miss out — it has Steinlager. The beer was invented in the city, it's brewed in the city, and a heck of an amount of it is drunk in the city. But Steinie drinkers might be shocked to discover that it was events in Wellington that led to their favourite beer brand coming into being.

The second Labour government came to power in 1957 — bear

with me here, it does involve beer! — and their finance minister, Arnold Nordmeyer, set about trying to solve a balance of payments crisis caused by the collapse of butter prices in Britain. Naturally, he didn't want to cut government spending, so he decided the only answer was to raise taxes. In what was to become known as the Black Budget, on 26 June 1958 Nordmeyer announced that he was going to increase the tax on beer, cigarettes, cars and petrol. And as if that wasn't bad enough he also threatened to cut imports of beer so people would buy the local product. There was a national outcry, as back then people loved nothing more than driving down to the pub to have a beer and a smoke with their mates.

Nordmeyer then challenged New Zealand brewers to come up with 'an international lager-style beer' so we didn't have to import quite so much. The good chaps at Lion Breweries decided to take Nordmeyer up on his challenge and soon began to market a new lager, known as Steinecker. The beer was named after the German manufacturer of the brewing gear they used at Lion.

Sales of the new beer were strong, but in 1962 the Dutch brewers Heineken challenged Lion's use of the name Steinecker. Apparently they thought it was a bit close to Heineken — hard to believe unless you've had so much of it you're slurring! As a result, Lion changed the name of Steinecker to Steinlager. Either way, it's still a Steinie.

The change of name made no difference to the beer's fans and sales continued to grow. In the early 70s it was so popular that the company started exporting to the United States. It then went on to win the international Les Amis du Vin award for three years in a row before being asked in 1980 not to enter again. They didn't. But in 1985 they did enter the Brewing Industry awards in England, as did

800 other beers. You guessed it! Steinlager was named the best beer in the world. Take that, Les Amis du Vin!

Fresh from their big win, the Steinlager team decided to take on a couple of other winners and began their long-term relationship with both the All Blacks and the New Zealand America's Cup team.

Over the years, the Steinlager range has expanded to include, briefly, Steinlager Blue, Steinlager Pure, Steinlager Light, and, to mark Sean Fitzpatrick's retirement from the All Blacks, there was even a limited-edition Seanlager produced! It doesn't get more Auckland that that . . .

Wohnsiedler

Wine's become awfully fashionable in this country over the last few years. Before the rise of the boutique vineyards of Marlborough, Martinborough and Central Otago, New Zealanders were pretty happy drinking a handful of wines whose names are now maligned — Velluto Rosso, Cook's Chasseur, Liebestraum and Wohnsiedler among them. While a number of these are still available, they're looked down upon by the winerati who at the same time overlook the important role these wines played in developing the industry as we know it today.

Take, for example, the Wohnsiedler name. You might think of it as a cask wine available for about the price of a bottle of 'cheap' Waipara riesling — but it's a whole lot more than that. Friedrich Wohnsiedler was one of the pioneers of wine-making in Gisborne.

Born in Germany in 1879, Friedrich Wohnsiedler grew up in

Baden Württemberg, where wine growing was a hobby for many local people, so you could say that he had wine in his veins! He came to New Zealand in his early twenties and got a job working in the meat industry. In 1907 he made a brief trip back to Europe, where he met the woman who would become his wife, Anna. They returned to New Zealand in 1910 and married shortly after. A couple of years later they moved to Gisborne where Friedrich opened a butchery on the main street.

Like many German migrants, Friedrich and his family were on the receiving end of considerable hostility with the onset of the First World War. This hostility culminated on New Year's Eve 1914 when a huge crowd wrecked the family's butchery. Friedrich, Anna and their three kids escaped out a window and across a neighbouring building — heaven knows what would have happened to them if they hadn't managed to get out.

Driven out of Gisborne, they moved to Matawhero where Friedrich worked on a farm. A couple of years later, they bought a small holding at Waihirere, about 13 kilometres north of Gisborne. The family finally moved to the land in 1921, once a house had been built and vineyards planted. At the time, most wine grapes were being grown by the Corbans and others in West Auckland, and also in Hawke's Bay. Wohnsiedler was one of the first to recognise the potential for growing grapes in Gisborne and Poverty Bay.

Waihirere was not only home to the vineyard, but it was also the brand name that Wohnsiedler chose for his produce, which was not restricted to wine — he also produced port, sherry and Madeira.

Wohnsiedler passed away in February 1958, leaving the Waihirere vineyard to his sons George and Fred. They continued to build the

company, buying grapes from neighbouring growers and investing in new machinery. The Wohnsiedler family eventually sold the vineyard to Montana Wines in 1973.

Monteith's

The discovery of gold on the West Coast of the South Island in 1864 drew thousands of people to the region, all of them there to make their fortunes. Many of them didn't find much of the actual gold that they were looking for, but they were pretty familiar with the golden liquid you could buy at the local pub. And boy, did they have choice — at the peak of the rushes there were more than 800 pubs on the West Coast, with 87 of them on one Hokitika street alone!

Within a couple of years 30,000 people had arrived on the coast, including the Monteith family. They settled in Reefton, and instead of searching for gold they started brewing beer and selling it to the miners. Their brewery, the Phoenix, first began producing beer in 1868. The recipe for their pale ale was so good that it lives on in Stewart Monteith's Original Ale.

The Phoenix Brewery continued to produce beer in Reefton until 1927 when Westland Breweries Ltd was formed from a bunch of Westland breweries — Pearn's of Kumara, both Mandl's and Davies Bros of Hokitika, as well as Phoenix. The new conglomeration of brewers set up their head office in Greymouth. The beers were then brewed in Kumara, Reefton and Hokitika, then taken to Greymouth for bottling.

This went on until the Kumara brewery closed in 1942. Brewing continued during the Second World War, but just when the war had ended and things were getting back to normal the brewing company had a bit of a bad year. In 1948 the Greymouth bottling plant was damaged in a fire, but worse, beer drinkers on the Coast boycotted the amber brew in protest at price rises! The boycott lasted an incredible three months before the temptation became too much and normal consumption resumed.

Over the next 40 years, beer production on the Coast consolidated in Greymouth. The Reefton brewery was closed in 1959, followed by the Hokitika brewery in 1967. In 1969 Dominion Breweries took over Westland Breweries, but production continued pretty much as usual.

In 1985 the brewery was developing new products and the brewers decided they needed to look backwards to go forwards — the result was the release of beers carrying the Monteith's brand. The move was a success, and by 1999 Monteith's had been voted Best Brewery in Australasia at the Australian International Brewing Awards.

The flush of success was to be short-lived on the coast, however. In 2001, DB Breweries announced that they were going to close the Monteith's Brewery and move the brand's brewing to Auckland. A worse insult to a West Coaster is almost unthinkable. Beer drinkers on the Coast and all over the country made their displeasure known and DB were forced to rethink their strategy. The brewery remains open to this day.

RETAIL THERAPY

7

Being such an inventive and entrepreneurial bunch of people, it's hardly surprising that New Zealanders are quite innovative when it comes to selling the stuff we make. And there's nothing like a little bit of retail therapy . . .

Four Square

There are about 300 Four Square foodstores throughout New Zealand. You've probably nipped into one recently to pick up some milk, a loaf of bread or a Sunday paper. In smaller places the Four Square is often the only grocery in town, so it becomes the hub of the community. In bigger cities, they're in convenient spots to pick up passing trade. Either way, the Four Square is a part of daily life for many New Zealanders.

The Four Square story goes back to 1922. An Auckland grocer called Mr J Heaton Barker noticed that chains of grocery stores were able to negotiate better deals with their suppliers than individual stores on their own. Heaton Barker was keen to equal this out a bit so he called a meeting of the Auckland Master Grocers Association on 6 July 1922. At the meeting Heaton Barker suggested that the city's independent grocers all get together and form a cooperative buying group. By doing this, they would still all own their own businesses but they would be able to buy goods at prices similar to those their larger competitors were getting.

The rest of the Master Grocers thought this was a great idea, and so a cooperative was born. It was to be a wee while before the group was registered as a company, but on 1 April 1925 Foodstuffs Ltd officially came into being. The Auckland cooperative started a trend that slowly moved down the country; a Wellington co-op was established in 1922, Christchurch took the idea on in 1928 and, lagging behind quite a bit, Dunedin hooked on to the co-op way of doing things in 1948.

With their cooperative set up, Heaton Barker and his cohorts decided they needed a new name for their buying group. One day

Barker was talking on the phone to another member of the buying group and doing what lots of people do when they're not really listening — doodling on his calendar. The doodle turned out to be the inspiration he was looking for. The date of that phone call was 4 July 1924 and Barker had drawn a square around the date. While this might seem kind of innocuous, Barker thought Four Square would be a great name for the buying group. Why? Because he reckoned together the group would 'stand Four Square to all winds that blew'.

By the end of that year the Four Square name had started to appear on the stores of some of the co-op members. The early branding featured red and gold panels with a '4' painted inside a square.

By the 1950s there were 700 Four Square stores up and down the country. It was around this time that the Foodstuffs group came up with their famous logo — the Four Square man. This grinning, thumbs-up grocer started life in newspaper advertising but soon became a fixture in all Four Square stores. New Zealanders became so fond of the Four Square man that a company has recently started producing a range of souvenirs featuring his image and Kiwis can't get enough of them!

Smith & Caughey's

The prestigious Auckland department store Smith & Caughey's sits regally on a whole city block of Queen St. It is an icon of the city that harks back to its more glamorous past. When imagining the founding of the store it's hard to go past the idea of a bewhiskered Mr Smith and a dapper Mr Caughey — well, there was a Mr Smith and a Mr Caughey, but the real driving force behind the establishment of the store was an Irish woman, Marianne Caughey.

Born in Portaferry, County Down in 1851, Marianne spent her early adulthood working for missions helping the poor of Belfast. At the age of 23 she married William Smith in Portaferry before doing what many young Irish people did at the time — sailing for

New York. The couple spent about four years there before returning briefly to Belfast.

In 1879 they sailed for New Zealand on the *Ben Nevis*, arriving in Auckland in January 1880. Within a very short time Marianne started Smith's Cheap Drapery Warehouse on Queen St (pictured) — the business was geographically close to the current Smith & Caughey's store but it was a million miles away from what the store would become. It worked on very tight margins and high turnover, with the motto 'A nimble sixpence rather than a slow shilling'.

In 1882 Marianne's brother, Andrew Caughey, arrived in Auckland and joined the business as a partner with William. Even though Marianne had started and built the company she was not a partner, a reflection of the expected roles of women in business at the time. It was at this point that the company's name was changed to Smith & Caughey's.

Two years later the store shifted across the road to the site where it still stands. The business continued to grow despite being on the unfashionably shady side of the street. Over the following 20 years Smith & Caughey's expanded along the block in line with the growth of the business. Marianne and William took several trips overseas to buy the latest and most fashionable goods for the store — at competitive prices. This upset local wholesalers, but it was a hit with the store's clientele.

Throughout her life in Auckland Marianne Smith continued the mission work she had started in Belfast. She was actively involved in the Helping Hand Mission, the forerunner to today's Methodist Central Mission. While she and her family had a flourishing business she never forgot the people less fortunate than herself.

In 1900 Marianne's role in the establishment of the company was finally acknowledged when Smith & Caughey's became a limited liability company with Marianne as one of the eight shareholders. She wouldn't become a director until four years after the death of her husband in 1912.

In 1916, Marianne Smith donated her home, The Grange in Herne Bay, to the Salvation Army for use as an orphanage for girls. Over the coming years she also donated a chapel to Wesley College, and Craigavon Park in Green Bay and Quinton Park on the North Shore were given to the city.

By the time Marianne Smith died in 1938 she had an estate worth £325,000 (the equivalent of about $29 million today). She left only £100 to the son she adopted in her late fifties, and the rest was put into a trust to continue her charitable works.

Long before she died, the day-to-day running of Smith & Caughey's had fallen to Andrew Caughey and his descendants. The fourth generation of the Caughey family continue to own and run the store today.

Foodtown

The concept of one-stop food markets was first introduced in the United States with the advent of King Kullen Market in Long Island, New York in 1930. The concept caught on in the States. In New Zealand, where the pace of life was a little slower and new-fangled ideas were viewed with more than a little suspicion, it took nearly 30 years before we got our first 'super' market.

For many Kiwis it's hard to imagine there was ever a time when you didn't jump in the car, drive down to your local supermarket, cruise into the carpark, drive around and around, curse the lack of parking places, finally find one that's so small you have to squeeze out of the passenger door, grab a trolley then do the entire week's shopping in one great big store. But there was a time when shopping was done at a variety of shops, with helpful grocers, butchers and greengrocers assisting you to select your purchases. In fact, getting your groceries usually meant giving your list to the grocer, who would go away and get all the products off the shelf for you!

This labour-intensive and time-consuming way of shopping was to be changed forever on 18 June 1958 in the Auckland suburb of Otahuhu. That was the day New Zealand's first supermarket opened. The men behind it, Tom Ah Chee, John Brown and Norman Kent, all had their own fruit and vegetable shops. They had noticed that as more and more people got cars, the weekly shopping would be done and then popped in the boot and driven home. If they offered carparking, making it easy to bring the family car and do the shopping, then surely that would attract more customers?

The men decided to take a risk and build a completely new kind of business, a supermarket they would call Foodtown. They each sold their own shops, and a big mortgage later the men bought a 1.1-hectare site on the outskirts of the main Otahuhu shopping area, not far from where a whole lot of new housing was being built in Otara. Being in quite a lot of debt, the business owners did quite a bit of work building their new 1400-square-metre market themselves. Can you imagine that now? The owners of new supermarkets rolling up their sleeves and doing a bit of concreting . . .

So uncertain of their new enterprise were the market's owners, they ensured that the design of their new building was such that it could easily be turned into a service station if the business went to pies!

They needn't have worried. The store's revolutionary new 118-space carpark was full within an hour of the store opening, and there was a traffic jam more than a kilometre long as people lined up to get into the store. Compare this with the opening of the new Sylvia Park mall not far away in Mt Wellington in 2006. The mall has some 3000 carparks but its opening still caused gridlock on the roads every which way.

Instead of advertising on the radio to attract customers to Foodtown, the owners had to call 1ZB and ask them to tell people to stay away until the next day, such was the chaos and clamour to get into this new store. The lucky few who made it inside got to pick their own groceries off the shelves, buy all their meat from chiller cabinets and select their own vegetables before taking it all to a checkout and paying for it. While the whole self-service thing was a novelty to customers, there was one service they still expected someone to do for them — Foodtown had to have staff on hand to carry customers' purchases to their cars and pop them in the boot!

The enterprise was such a success that within two years a second Foodtown had opened in Takanini. There are now 30 Foodtown supermarkets around the North Island and the company that owns them, Progressive Enterprises, also owns the Woolworths and Countdown stores. And now you have to put your own groceries in the boot.

Arthur Barnett

It's hard to imagine Dunedin's night sky without the neon sign of a running horse atop the Arthur Barnett store. The horse was one of the first 40 neon signs in the country when it was installed in 1930. Although it's known locally as Arthur Barnett's horse, not many people know that the horse's rider is in fact a likeness of Arthur Barnett himself, the horse running so fast that Barnett's hat is being blown away in the wind. The horse too has a name — Can't Stop! And it would seem the name is appropriate — when the department store burnt down in 1959 with damage estimated at £1 million, Can't Stop survived.

By the time Can't Stop was erected, his rider was already 57 and had owned his own business for 27 years. Arthur Barnett was born in Dunedin in 1873. He left school in 1887 and took up an apprenticeship in the drapery trade with A&T Inglis, one of the first large stores to set up business north of the Octagon. At the age of 27 he decided that he wanted to set up his own store — a dream that became reality in 1903.

The first Arthur Barnett store was at 100 George St, offering high-grade gents' ties, gloves, braces, shirts and collars. Barnett opened his store amid stiff competition but he was determined to offer the best quality at the lowest prices. In his first year in business, he managed to turn a £160 profit and employ his first staff member.

In 1909, business was going so well that the company moved to a larger site — where the store still stands today. Their shifting sale promised '£5000 worth of goods to the slaughter, and only a few weeks in which to do the killing'!

In order to fund the store's expansion, Arthur Barnett became a limited liability company. The expanding store soon offered mail order facilities for country customers, and long shopping hours.

It wasn't until the 1920s that the Arthur Barnett we know today started to emerge. It was during that decade that the store made its first steps to becoming a department store. More stock required more space, and the building programme resulted in the opening of a newly built store in 1925 — the facade of which is still standing today. The following year the company posted a profit of £71,000, the equivalent of nearly $6 million today.

Like many of the big department stores, Arthur Barnett sales are famous. So popular were they in the 1950s, that when word got out that Arthur Barnett pants were down again, people would flock to the store for cheap kecks!

Business continued strongly over the next few decades, despite the shortages caused by the Second World War. The years following the war saw the company continue to grow. However, it was struck a double blow in 1959. The first was the death of the store's founder at the age of 86 on 10 February. Arthur's sons, Jeffrey and Arthur, had already taken over running the business in the early 1950s but Arthur was still often to be found in the store — especially enjoying pretending to be the lift attendant. Can you imagine what those customers would have thought if they'd realised it was Arthur Barnett himself pressing the lift buttons for them?

The second blow was a massive fire on 9 December. What started as a small fire in the basement in the early evening took hold, and despite the best efforts of fire crews from all over the city, within two hours of the alarms going off at 7.49pm the store was doomed. Incredibly there were no casualties — and the store's facade and Can't Stop were rescued. Equally incredibly, within five months the store had been rebuilt and was back in business, bigger and better. It stayed pretty much the same until another massive revamp in the 1990s, and in 1997 Arthur Barnett opened in the Meridian Mall, which is where the store can be found today.

MADE IN NEW ZEALAND

Kirkcaldie & Stains

Today's grande dame of the Wellington shopping scene, Kirkcaldie & Stains, is about as glamorous as shopping in the city gets. The store, replete with its chandeliers, grand piano and alluring window displays, couldn't be further from where it started as little more than a shed on the beach!

OK, so that beach was Lambton Quay and the site was where the historic Bank of New Zealand building now stands, but the earliest Kirkcaldie & Stains store was very basic. Since then, the shoreline has been pushed a couple of blocks away from Lambton Quay and the store has moved to its more upmarket premises a bit further down the road.

John Kirkcaldie was born in Scotland in 1838. He started a draper's apprenticeship there at the age of 12. The work was hard and the hours were long, so as soon as he reached the age of 19 he left Scotland, settling first in Ireland, then England and then making the journey to Australia. It was in Sydney in 1861 that he became acquainted with his soon-to-be business partner, Robert Stains. The same age as Kirkcaldie, Stains was born in Dartford in the English county of Kent. He had also taken a draper's apprenticeship in his youth, then spent some years plying his trade in London. The pair had met in London, but it was not until Stains also moved to Sydney that he and Kirkcaldie became friends.

The pair decided to go into business together and pooled their funds. But Sydney was oversupplied with drapers, so where to go? A friend who was already in Nelson recommended they try Wellington or Christchurch. They knew of a draper already in Christchurch, so Wellington it was.

The pair arrived in winter 1863 and soon set about finding suitable premises for their new enterprise. The best they could afford was a small building on Lambton Quay that had been built from the timbers of the wrecked ship *Inconstant*. Parts of the ship, now known as Plimmer's Ark, can be seen in the Old Bank Arcade on the site of the original Kirkcaldie & Stains store.

MADE IN NEW ZEALAND

Stock was bought from contacts in Sydney and the shop was soon opened. The pair's promise of the latest fashions at good prices saw the business become a success. By 1868 they needed larger premises so they moved to a section of reclaimed land which was close to the port. That piece of land was on the corner of Lambton Quay and Brandon St, a block of the city that Kirkcaldie & Stains has since made its own.

Life went on for Messrs Kirkcaldie and Stains. They both married in 1870 and soon after started families. Things went on as normal until the 1880s, which were tough years in the drapery business as the economy took a downturn. Pressure on the business culminated in Robert Stains deciding to leave the partnership and return to his native England. The Kirkcaldie family continued to run the store, rebuilding in 1908, including the facade that is still the hallmark of the company today. The depression of the early 1930s saw the end of the Kirkcaldie family's ownership of the store, and it was bought by an English company in 1931.

Ballantynes

A visit to Ballantynes department store is as much a part of Christchurch's heritage as a trip on the city's historic tram, a cruise down the Avon on a punt or a visit to Cathedral Square. Although the company changed its name a few times in the early years, one thing about Ballantynes has always remained the same — its presence on Cashel St.

In the 1850s Christchurch was a tiny fraction of the size of the sprawling city you see today. The first settlers to arrive in the new church settlement made their way across the Port Hills from Lyttelton in 1850. The ninth ship to deliver settlers, the *Labuan*, arrived at Lyttelton on 14 August 1851. It carried the founders of the original Ballantynes store, David Clarkson, his wife Esther, and his sister Elizabeth. In Lyttelton, David soon went to work as a builder and his wife and sister put their millinery skills to good use.

In 1853 the family decided to move across the hill to Christchurch. They soon found and bought a small cottage on Cashel St, from which Esther began selling hats and other imported clothing. When David saw how well this real cottage business was doing, he built a small shop for his wife in front of the house.

Along with David's cousin Thomas Atkinson, the Clarksons decided to expand their business. They leased a second property on Cashel St and took a buying trip to Australia. With stock and premises sorted, an advertisement appeared in the *Lyttelton Times* on 23 September 1854 extolling 'a new drapery establishment . . . with an entirely new and extensive stock of drapery, boots, shoes etc'.

Thomas Atkinson left the partnership in 1856 but this didn't seem to put a damper on the development of the store. The same year, the shop was extended and was officially named Dunstable House — in acknowledgement of Esther's home town in the English country of Bedfordshire. Business boomed and the Clarksons continued to expand their range of goods, working hard in the shop until 6 July 1863. That was the date on which William Pratt took over the business. Elizabeth Clarkson continued working for him to ensure a smooth handover, but Pratt scarcely needed it as he already had a successful general store in Lyttelton.

Pratt set about expanding the building and the business. And then along came Ballantyne — John Ballantyne. He was a Scotsman from Selkirk who had emigrated to Australia in 1852. He had set up his own drapery business in Adelaide but didn't enjoy that city's climate so decided to move to Christchurch, which had a climate much more becoming of a Scotsman!

In 1872, Ballantyne and his family arrived in Christchurch with the proceeds of the sale of his business in South Australia. He went looking for a business to buy and soon set his sights on Dunstable House. William Pratt's sons weren't interested in taking over the business so he decided to sell it to Ballantyne. An advertisement announcing the sale appeared in *The Press* on 20 June 1872, stating 'Referring to the above, Dunstable House will in future be conducted under the style or firm of J. Ballantyne and Co'.

And style was the key for the store under Ballantyne's reign. He knew that to stay ahead of his competitors he had to keep in step with fashion. He also believed strongly in the power of advertising, and ads for the store were a regular feature in the city's newspapers.

Ballantyne ran the company until 1879 when he retired to a family farm near Mt Peel in the Rangitata district. The Ballantyne name lived on, however, as his son Josiah Ballantyne took over running the family business along with a number of business partners. And so a precedent was set for the generations of Ballantynes to come — since John Ballantyne retired from the store there has always been a Ballantyne at the head of the company.

VISITORS FROM OVERSEAS

8

Even though New Zealanders have invented heaps of good stuff, there are still a few products from overseas that we love so much we've come to think of them as our own.

Maggi onion soup

It's been on our supermarket shelves since 1952, it's one of this country's best-selling soup mixes, and most New Zealanders have never tasted the soup. Hard to believe? Not when Maggi onion soup is the mix in question.

Ever since the following recipe appeared in magazines in the 1960s, Kiwis haven't been able to get enough of it:

Quick Savoury Dip or Spread
— just mix and it's made

- Half packet of Maggi onion soup
- One tin (4 oz) Nestlé's reduced cream
- One and a half teaspoons of lemon juice or half teaspoon of vinegar

Mix all ingredients together and place in refrigerator for at least two hours before using. Will keep for a week in the refrigerator.

The ladies of the Nestlé home economics service test kitchen can't have begun to imagine that this dip recipe would become so much a part of New Zealand culinary lore that it's probably the only recipe most of us know off by heart!

While the recipe might be as Kiwi as it gets, the company that makes the classic soup mix was actually started in 1872 in Switzerland. Perhaps unsurprisingly, the man who started the company was called

Julius Maggi. Possessed of an inventive streak, Maggi took over his father's mill at the age of 26. He then set about establishing a food production business.

The industrial revolution meant that the lives of working people in Europe had changed massively over the previous century. With increased industrialisation, longer working hours and a decreased profitability of small farms, the diet of working families suffered. Julius Maggi decided to try to do something about this by inventing something that would improve the nutritional value of the food that they did have.

In 1883, Maggi worked with a local doctor to develop a dried pea and bean soup mix. The soup was quick to prepare and highly nutritious. By 1886, the company had released a further three soup flavours and Maggi was working on some new products. One of these was Maggi wurze — or Maggi spice. This sauce, which was designed as a substitute for meat extracts, is still found in many Swiss and German kitchens today.

While Mr Maggi was busy inventing soups, the company that would eventually bring his products to New Zealand, Nestlé, registered its trademark in Wellington in 1885. It took another 62 years before the Maggi brand arrived in the country, but it didn't take long to make itself right at home.

Jaffas

Jaffas used to be synonymous with Friday night at the movies, where they'd make a heck of a noise when rolled down the uncarpeted aisles of the local fleapit. That was until some wag decided that Jaffa stood for Just Another F***ing Aucklander. Well, it might come as a surprise to find that our beloved little orange lolly was first made by Just Another Foodie Australian!

James Stedman, the grandson of a convict Englishman, was born in Sydney in 1860. He worked for his father, who had been a confectioner since the age of 14. The Stedmans were pretty good at making lollies, as by 1889 the company was making five tons of sweets a week.

In the early 1900s, James Stedman Ltd was producing traditional boiled sweets and doing very well thank you. When James's father died in 1913, he took over the company and the future happiness of New Zealand lolly-lovers was secured. In 1931, James Stedman Ltd released the Jaffa on the New Zealand and Australian markets. The rest, as they say, is history.

While Jaffas originally came from Australia, their name came from much further afield. It comes all the way from the Middle East.

Jaffa is now a borough of the city of Tel Aviv in Israel, but it used to be a city in its own right. It's so old that it's mentioned in the Bible, not once, not twice but four times. There are quite a few theories about where the name Jaffa came from. The one Kiwis will probably agree with is that Yofi in Hebrew means beauty, and we all know that our Jaffas really are beauties!

So how do we get from a port town in Israel to a confection in

New Zealand? Well, the lolly's orange flavour and round shape meant that it made sense to name it after a type of orange. After Vasco da Gama brought oranges to Europe from China in the sixteenth century, the sweet fruit soon became established throughout the world. One variety of really sweet orange thrived in the soils of Palestine and, later, Israel. That orange then became known by the name of one of the towns it grew near — Jaffa.

Vegemite

New Zealanders don't have a reputation for being adventurous eaters, but there's one Kiwi delicacy that we love which the rest of the world (our near-neighbours excluded) just can't understand. Such is the fear of this product that rumours abounded a couple of years ago that it had been banned in the United States. What could possibly cause such a stirring of passions? — simple, it's good old Vegemite.

Many a Kiwi breakfast table is graced with that yellow-lidded jar of salty brown spread. In fact, there are plenty of us who couldn't possibly start the day without it. Like a lot of our favourite products, Vegemite originated in Australia (but it's ok because we've still got the pavlova, Phar Lap and Split Enz!).

The Vegemite story goes back to 1922 when Fred Walker — of the Fred Walker Company — hired an industrial chemist called Cyril Callister to come up with a way of making a spread out of brewer's yeast. The yeast is incredibly high in vitamin B, so Callister's challenge was to make something that was not only tasty but healthy as well.

Callister set to work and soon came up with a spreadable product that tasted pretty good. It was then sold into stores under the name Pure Vegetable Extract. While that's what was in the jar, it was a bit of a marketing own-goal. Imagine breakfast tables across Australasia — 'Honey, do you want Pure Vegetable Extract or jam on your toast?' It doesn't really work, does it?

Fred Walker decided that if the product was going to take off it needed a better name. Using a slightly sharper marketing strategy he held a nationwide competition to name the product, with a prize of 50 pounds to the winner. Who that was is lost in the mists of time, but the name Vegemite, thankfully, isn't.

Vegemite was first seen on Australian shelves in 1923, and it was described as 'delicious on sandwiches and toast, and improves the flavours of soups, stews and gravies'. It sounds as if nothing much has changed!

It wasn't love at first sight for Australian toast munchers though. The product was up against some tough competition from Marmite, which was imported from England. Like many things, consumers thought that the product from the 'home country' must be superior to the locally made one. To try and counter this, in 1928 Fred Walker changed the name of Vegemite. The new name — Parwill. Parwill? What? Think about it — if Marmite then Parwill!

This name lasted nearly ten years until Walker decided to go back to Vegemite and try and make it work. The company held a massive marketing drive, giving away prizes and getting the name Vegemite out there. They succeeded, and the spread thrived in both Australia and New Zealand.

Electrolux vacuum cleaners

Had it not been for a company merger in Sweden in 1919, New Zealanders would now be keeping their carpets clean by doing a spot of mekaniskaing. This was the year in which a company called Elektromekamiska AB merged with another company called Lux AB and thus was born Elektrolux. Kiwis have taken to the brand so much that instead of doing the vacuuming, we now talk about doing the luxing.

While we've taken the Electrolux brand — the 'c' was added in 1957 — into our lexicon, the product itself is a very Swedish one. The first nugget of an idea to make vacuum-cleaning technology available to every household came to Swedish salesman Axel Wenner-Gren as he was strolling down a Viennese street in 1908. In a shop window he saw a big 20-kilogram American vacuum cleaner for sale. (Imagine lugging that around while you do the carpets!) The machine was priced at around the equivalent of NZ$4500.

Wenner-Gren had a light-bulb moment. He realised that if he could make a vacuum cleaner lighter and cheaper, then everyone would want one. And he was right. Within a couple of years he got a job working for a company that was manufacturing these huge vacuum cleaners. He managed to convince the company that the product should be lighter and cheaper, so they reduced the weight by six kilograms and nearly halved the price. This wasn't enough for Wenner-Gren.

He contacted a Swedish designer, who came up with a portable, light and easily manufactured vacuum, and Wenner-Gren set up his own company to manufacture it. The new machine went down a storm. Such was its success that Wenner-Gren bought a share of

Old fashioned Cleaning Methods are DANGEROUS

Whenever you flick a duster or move a broom—you release countless disease-laden germs within your home.

Whenever you stand on a chair to dust a picture—move a heavy couch or table—you take the risk of a fall or a strain.

The old ideas of home cleaning are very dangerous. Hospitals can relate thousands of stories of suffering women—injured by their own folly in clinging to old-fashioned methods.

Think of your own health and strength. Think of the health of your family.

Make yours a SAFER, HEALTHIER, HAPPIER HOME

Electrolux brings you easy, pleasant, satisfactory house-cleaning—inexpensively. Saves hours of useless and physically injurious drudgery —makes ample leisure for your pleasures. Gives healthy, dust-free homes. Saves money by its many varied uses.

Electrolux is the most modern type of vacuum cleaner. It is the most effective, and the simplest to operate. There is no heavy outside dust bag to drag about. Various extension fittings make every cleaning job easy to do—thoroughly and healthfully.

FROM

£13-5-0

You can secure Electrolux easily. Its cost is low—its value without measure. You will prove it indispensable in your home. Write or telephone if you would like further details of the modern Electrolux method of protecting your health and happiness.

ELECTROLUX
ELECTROLUX LIMITED
Auckland: 47-49 Customs St. East. Christchurch: 639 Colombo St. Dunedin: 169 Rattray St. Invercargill: 46A Esk St. Wellington: 15 Manners St. New Plymouth: Egmont St. Palmerston North: 95 Cuba Street. Timaru: 257 Stafford St. Hamilton: 79 Victoria Street.

MADE IN NEW ZEALAND

the Swedish manufacturing company Elektromekaniska, which later merged with Lux (Lux, by the way, is Latin for light).

Ever the salesman, the lux man knew he had to take the product to the international market to really make money from it. By 1919 Elektroluxes were being sold throughout Europe. It was a wee bit longer before the cleaners appeared downunder, with an Australian production plant opening in 1936.

Such was our enthusiasm for the Elektrolux, not even the Second World War could prevent the opening of a manufacturing plant in New Zealand. The first Kiwi-made Lux rolled off the production line in 1940 and before long we were luxing instead of vacuuming.

While Kiwis have taken the Lux into our language, South Africans have gone one better. They've named a species of marine ray after their favourite vacuum cleaner. The *Electrolux addisoni* lives in the Indian Ocean off the South African coast. The reason for its unusual name? It's an electric ray that feeds using a vigorous sucking action!

Kiwi shoe polish

Tell someone from overseas who is not familiar with our fine nation that you're a Kiwi and they might think you're telling them you're a furry green fruit or a tin of shoe polish. The Kiwi/kiwifruit confusion is understandable, given that a lot of countries have dropped the fruit part of the name. But the boot polish — where does that come from?

Unlike many of the international products that we've taken to our hearts in this country, the invention of Kiwi polish does actually have a New Zealand link — and don't worry, none of our national

birds are harmed in the making of this fine product!

The Kiwi polish story starts with a Scotsman called William Ramsay. The Ramsay family moved from Scotland to Melbourne in 1878 when William was ten years old. After leaving school William joined his father's real estate business, taking advantage of Melbourne's booming real estate industry.

In 1900, Ramsay made a fortuitous visit to New Zealand — fortuitous as this is where he met his wife Annie Elizabeth Meek. They married among the majestic whitestone buildings of her home town, Oamaru, on 2 January 1901 — saving Ramsay from ever having to make a New Year's resolution to remember their wedding anniversary!

Before long the pair moved back to Melbourne and William went into business with a chap called Hamilton McKellar. The pair, rather predictably, called their new company Ramsay & McKellar. They set about manufacturing stove polish, boot cream and disinfectant.

In 1906, the pair decided to launch a new brand of boot polish, having had minor success with one called Mirror. This time they wanted a catchy name for the brand — something that would stand out. As a nod to Mrs Ramsay's New Zealand origins, they settled on the name Kiwi, with packaging that featured our national bird front and centre.

While it might seem a bit strange to name a boot polish after a flightless bird from another country, the brand took off (if you'll excuse the pun . . .). Within six years Kiwi was the top-selling brand of polish in the whole of Australia. It was time to take on the world, and Kiwi polish was introduced in England. Ramsay died two years later but the brand continued to go from strength to strength.

While the manufacture of a lot of products was halted because

of the First World War, the Kiwi polish factories carried on at full steam as the Australian, British and American forces all used the polish on their marching boots. In its first 12 years of production a staggering 30 million tins of Kiwi were sold.

Since then Kiwi has gone on to become one of the most used shoe polishes in 180 countries. Now owned by the Sara Lee Corporation, the brand with our flightless bird on the tin holds a whopping 65 per cent market share in the United States, where it is advertised using such witty slogans as: 'Raise your chance of dating a supermodel from 0 to 0.001'.

Milo

When Milo was first made in New Zealand in 1940, it was promoted as a fortified tonic food that would induce peaceful sleep. In the intervening years it's become our favourite chocolate energy drink, and instead of sending us off to the land of nod, it now helps thousands of Kiwis to 'get more go'!

Because we've been drinking it for over 70 years, a lot of New Zealanders think of the delicious chocolatey drink as one of our own products. While the first Milo made in New Zealand was produced at the Underwood dairy factory just out of Invercargill, the original product was invented in Australia. Milo first made its way across the Tasman in 1935 and Kiwis drank the Aussie brew for five years until manufacturing began on our own fair shores.

When it first arrived here, Milo was a mere one year old. It's always been produced by Nestlé, and it was at the Nestlé factory in Smithtown,

New South Wales that it was invented. The Nestlé company had been trying to come up with a dried powder that could be added to milk or water to make a chocolate energy drink. They hit a bit of a snag when they couldn't work out how to make the drink-mix dry enough that it wouldn't go lumpy if it was stored in a tin for a while.

In 1933, an industrial chemist working for Nestlé, Thomas Mayne, hit on the idea of using recently developed vacuum-drying technology to get all of the moisture out of the drink powder. Mayne's innovation was the breakthrough the Milo makers needed, and the drink was launched at Sydney's Royal Easter Show the following year. It was an instant success and the brand has continued to grow ever since. It is now sold in over 30 countries as varied as Singapore, Indonesia and Ghana, where it tends to be mixed with water instead of milk. In Malaysia, it's even used as filling for roti bread instead of jam. If you prefer the liquid milky version you can buy it in cans from vending machines in Hong Kong.

The brand Milo has become well-established since the 1930s, but the original Milo that the product was named after is much, much older. Even though Milo was advertised as helping you get a good night's sleep, the people at Nestlé knew that their product would help kids build muscle and get stronger. They looked back to the classical world and came across a Greek character called Milo of Croton.

This resident of Croton in Italy lived in the sixth century BC. Even though he was from Italy, it was in Greece that he became famous. He was a tremendous athlete who was crowned as the champion of the Ancient Olympics a massive six times!

Cattle-carrying seems to have been a bit of a hobby for Milo, as it's said that as soon as the Olympics had finished he would start training for the next games. He would buy a small calf and train by carrying the calf around on his shoulders. By the time the games came around again he'd be carrying a four-year-old cattle beast on his shoulders — an extraordinary feat that was commemorated on the labels of early Milo tins.

La-Z-Boy chairs

Generations of New Zealanders have grown up with dads who like nothing more than to park up in their La-Z-Boy recliner chair, having a quiet beer, perusing the weekend's race cards and watching a bit of rugby on the telly.

The New Zealand manufacturers of the famous recliner reckon they've sold more La-Z-Boys than there are houses in New Zealand — that's how much we love these chairs. And admit it, you know the old jingle off by heart, so feel free to sing along: 'You can rock it, you can roll it, you can lock the rock and put your feet up, so sit right back and really enjoy the genuine La-Z-Boy!'

Even though we love the La-Z-Boy we can't lay claim to it. The first La-Z-Boy was invented in a small town called Monroe, in Michigan, in the United States. The chairs were the brainchild of the extraordinarily named cousins Edwin J. Shoemaker and Edward M. Knabusch.

Going into partnership in a furniture-making business, the cousins set out to make a chair that they thought was 'nature's way of relaxing'. In 1927, the pair came across a cunning idea that no-one had ever thought of when it came to chair building — they decided that their chair would recline.

The chair's link to nature was so strong that it was initially built as an outdoor chair made from wooden slats. People could now sit on their porch and recline on their nameless new chair as they contemplated the outdoor world. But the innovation didn't stop there.

Knabusch and Shoemaker realised that the outdoor chair was so good that maybe it should be moved indoors. So they padded it and upholstered it and took it inside, marketing it as a 'year round chair'. Not the most catchy brand name ever!

To find a more appropriate name for the chair, they did something cunning. They combined the need for a name with a marketing campaign and held a public competition to come up with a new name for their year-round chair.

The competition threw up some classic names, Slack Back and Sit-N-Snooze among them, but the ultimate winner was the name we know today — La-Z-Boy.

Heaps of Americans spent the next 40 years locking the rock and putting their feet up, but it wasn't until 1968 that the La-Z-Boy came to be manufactured in New Zealand. The company that makes them here, Morgan Furniture, was established in Auckland in 1944 and is still family owned and run. The Morgans met a representative of the Australian manufacturers of La-Z-Boys at the Easter Show in Auckland, and soon after they got the licence to manufacture the chairs here in New Zealand. They've been turning out our favourite rockers ever since. In fact, they've been so successful at it that in the 1990s they bought out the Australian company that first introduced them to the La-Z-Boy, and Morgan's now export the recliners to Australia!

Sunlight soap

If you've got dirty clothes, chances are you hiff them in the washing machine, chuck in a bit of washing powder and never give a second thought to them until it's time to hang them on the clothesline (or chuck them in the dryer, if you're a global-warming doubter!).

The kind of mechanical convenience that a washing machine provides would have been a dream to Kiwi housewives in the nineteenth century. Back then doing the washing more often than not involved boiling water in a copper out in the washhouse, and then washing all the clothes by hand in the hot water. And this could only be done on one day of the week — usually Monday — for having washing drying on the line on any other day could only cause the neighbours to suspect shoddy housekeeping at best, and league with the devil at worst!

Back then most people didn't even buy soap. Housewives used to make their own from animal fat, ash and goodness knows what else.

It's not hard to understand why housewives the country over took to a new laundry soap that was good quality, affordable and very very yellow! When Sunlight laundry soap arrived in New Zealand in the 1880s it became a household name very quickly.

The Sunlight brand became so well-loved that many Kiwis think of it as one of our own. Sadly, it's not — it's English. The soap was initially imported from the Sunlight factory at Port Sunlight near Liverpool, in the north of England. Yep, the town was named after the soap! The company making the soap was owned by a forward-thinking businessman called William Lever.

Lever started the company by selling precut, prewrapped soap

bars in his father's shop. He realised that he was on to something and started a soap factory. Lever was also quite revolutionary, only using vegetable oils instead of animal products in his soap. This meant that the soap lathered more easily and wasn't quite so smelly.

The first Sunlight soap was produced in 1884, and it was soon being exported to Australia and New Zealand. By 1888, Sunlight soap was so popular around the world that Lever & Co was making a massive 457 tonnes of it a week at its factory at Port Sunlight.

Lever knew that the way to get the best out of his workers was to treat them well, so he built the town of Port Sunlight so the workers would have safe, affordable housing, leisure facilities and other amenities.

By 1906, New Zealand's Sunlight soap was being made in Australia — but only until 1919 when William Lever chose a site for New Zealand's very own Sunlight soap factory at Petone in Wellington. The successor to Lever & Co, Unilever, still has a site in Petone today.

Cadbury

A young Englishman called John Cadbury opened a small grocery shop in Bull St, Birmingham in 1824. It might not have seemed like such a big thing at the time, but that little shop was the first step in developing an international business that would see John Cadbury's surname come to mean one thing the world over — chocolate.

After a few years in the grocery trade Cadbury decided to start manufacturing drinking chocolate and cocoa, which were fashionable

drinks at the time. By 1847, the company was big enough that John's brother Benjamin joined him. The chocolate boom continued, and in 1860 John's sons Richard and George took over the business. They carried on their father's work building the company, ensuring consistent good quality and selling heaps of chocolatey goodness.

In 1879, the Cadburys moved their whole factory to the outskirts of Birmingham, to an area called Bournville. They soon built an entire model village there for their workers, to provide them with good

housing, plenty of facilities for sport and entertainment — everything but a pub — the Cadbury family were Quakers and didn't approve of the drink.

Meanwhile, on the other side of the world, an entirely different tale was unfolding — the two stories to bisect a few decades later. In 1865, a young Englishman by the name of Daniel Bullock landed in Lyttelton. He had come to New Zealand drawn by the goldfields and the hope of a new life. Back in England he had worked on the railways, but more importantly he'd also worked in bread and biscuit baking.

To come to New Zealand he took a seaman's apprenticeship on a ship sailing out of Bristol. On arrival in Lyttelton, the 24-year-old left the ship and his English life behind. He headed north to the Pelorus goldfield but didn't make his fortune, so he returned south.

At some point around this time Daniel Bullock, gold prospector, became Richard Hudson, gentleman baker. One theory is that it was because he'd jumped ship and didn't want to be found as he was an illegal immigrant. Another has it that he spent time in hospital and renamed himself in gratitude to a doctor who helped save him. Whatever the truth is, Hudson and his wife Mary Ann moved to Dunedin in 1868.

Hudson soon set up a small baker's shop in Princes St. After a while he became renowned for the quality of the biscuits he made. So popular were his bickies that he stopped making bread. Before long, though, Hudson decided that sweets would be a good sideline for his biscuit factory, and he started producing confectionery too.

Hudson visited Europe in 1885 where he bought the machinery to produce cocoa and chocolate. Upon his return to Dunedin he put

this new technology to good use, manufacturing what is thought to have been the first chocolate in the southern hemisphere.

The year 1903 was a terrible one, as first the Hudson factory burnt down, then just ten months later the company's founder died. Hudson's biscuit and chocolate manufacturing continued, however, until in 1930 the company aligned itself with Cadbury to form Cadbury Fry Hudson. In 1969 the company merged with Schweppes, becoming Cadbury Schweppes Hudson. The Hudson name finally disappeared in 1990, when Cadbury sold the Hudson biscuit lines to Griffin's, who still make many of the old Hudson favourites — Toffee Pops, Shrewsburys and Sultana Pasties among them.

Griffin's also bought one of the country's favourite mascots, Chocolate Chippies' Cookie Bear, and his famous Dum-Dee-Doo greeting!

Bibliography

Books

Barnett, Stephen & Wolfe, Richard, *New Zealand! New Zealand! In praise of Kiwiana*, Penguin Books, Auckland, 1999

——, *Kiwiana: The sequel*, Penguin Books, Auckland, 2001

Barringer, EE, *Sweet Success: The story of Cadbury & Hudson in New Zealand*, Cadbury Confectionery Ltd, Dunedin, 2000

Bell, Claudia & Lyall, John, *Putting our Town on the Map: Local claims to fame in New Zealand*, HarperCollins, Auckland, 1995

Bridges, John & Downes, David, *No 8 Wire: The best of Kiwi ingenuity*, Hodder Moa Beckett, Auckland, 2000

Conly, Geoff, *Wattie's: The first fifty years*, J Wattie Canneries, Hastings, 1984

Cotter, MJ, *From Gold to Green: Paeroa and district 1875–1975*, Paeroa Borough Council, Paeroa, 1975

Crozier, Guyon, *If It's Made of Rubber: Para 75 years*, Para Rubber Co Ltd, Christchurch, 1985

Cryer, Max, *The Godzone Dictionary of Favourite New Zealand Words and Phrases*, Exisle, Auckland, 2006

Geary, Cecilie, *Smith and Caughey's: Celebrating 125 years, 1880–2005*, Smith & Caughey's Ltd, Auckland, 2005

Gordon, D, Speight's: The story of Dunedin's historic brewery, Avon Publishers, Dunedin, 1993

Haddon, Kathy, *Birkenhead: The way we were*, Birkenhead Library, North Shore City Council, Auckland, 1993

Irving, David & Inkson, Kerr, *It Must Be Wattie's: From Kiwi icon to global player*, David Bateman, Auckland, 1998

McLauchlan, Gordon, *The Story of Beer: Beer and brewing — a New Zealand history*, Penguin Books, Auckland, 1994

Millen, J, *Glaxo: From Joseph Nathan to Glaxo Wellcome*, Glaxo New Zealand Ltd, Palmerston North, 1991

——, *Kirkcaldie & Stains: A Wellington story*, Bridget Williams Books, Wellington, 2000

Nestlé New Zealand, *Family Matters: 120 years of Nestlé in New Zealand*, Nestlé New Zealand, Auckland 2006

New Zealand's Favourite Brands, New Zealand's Favourite Brands Ltd, Sydney 2004

Ogilvie, Gordon, *Ballantynes: The story of Dunstable House, 1854–2004*, Caxton Press, Christchurch, 2004

Price, Felicity, *LWR: 100 years in the making*, Hazard Press, Christchurch 2005

Reed, AH, *The Reed Dictionary of New Zealand Place Names*, Reed Publishing, Auckland, 2002

Ringer Monk, Valerie, *Crown Lynn: New Zealand icon*, Penguin Books, Auckland, 2006

Scott, Dick, *Pioneers of New Zealand Wine*, Reed Books, Auckland, 2002

Wolfe, Richard, *Well Made New Zealand: A century of trademarks*, Reed Methuen, Auckland, 1987

Articles

Barlow, Hugh, 'Art deco tower inspires devotion', *Wairarapa Times Age*, 21 April 2001

Bartle, Rhonda, 'One size fits all — the Swanndri success story', www.pukeariki.com

Bond, Georgina & Dann, Liam, 'They've got the look at House of G',

New Zealand Herald, Auckland, 1 April 2006

Boyd, Mary, 'Wattie, James 1902–1974', *Dictionary of New Zealand Biography*, updated 22 June 2007, www.dnzb.govt.nz

Coney, Sandra, 'Smith, Marianne 1851–1938', *Dictionary of New Zealand Biography*, updated 22 June 2007, www.dnzb.govt.nz

Cooper, Michael, 'Wohnsiedler, Friedrich 1879–1958', *Dictionary of New Zealand Biography*, updated 22 June 2007, www.dnzb.govt.nz

Crittenden, Victor, 'Yates, Arthur (1861–1926)', *Australian Dictionary of Biography*, Supplementary Volume, Melbourne University Press, 2005

Elliot, Stuart, 'Kiwi shoe polish aims to escape invisibility', *New York Times*, 14 December 2004

Fleming, JF, 'Fleming, Thomas 1848–1930', *Dictionary of New Zealand Biography*, updated 22 June 2007, www.dnzb.govt.nz

Gordon, Donald, 'Speight, Charles 1865–1928', *Dictionary of New Zealand Biography*, updated 22 June 2007, www.dnzb.govt.nz

Griggs, Geoff, 'European brews that will win over Kiwis', *Marlborough Express*, 21 February 2008

Howells, Shelley, 'Pretty in Pink', *New Zealand Heritage*, New Zealand Historic Places Trust, issue 103, Summer 2006.

Langmore, Diane, 'Ramsay, William (1868–1914)', *Australian Dictionary of Biography*, Volume 11, Melbourne University Press, 1988

Law, Tina, 'Iconic NZ outdoor firm Fairydown revived', *The Press*, 7 November 2007

Millen, Julia, 'Nathan, Joseph Edward 1835–1912', *Dictionary of New Zealand Biography*, updated 22 June 2007, www.dnzb.govt.nz

Owens, Peter, 'Nice one Jimmy!', *New Zealand Business*, November 2004

Palmer, Harriet, 'New claims rock jandal orthodoxy', *Taranaki Daily News*, 29 November 2007

Parry, Gordon, 'Hallenstein, Bendix 1835–1905', *Dictionary of New Zealand Biography*, updated 22 June 2007, www.dnzb.govt.nz

Walsh, GP, 'Stedman, James (1840–1913)', *Australian Dictionary of Biography*, Volume 12, Melbourne University Press, 1990

Winder, Virginia, 'Yarrows: How to earn a wholesome crust', Taranaki Stories, www.pukeariki.com

Withington, Barbara, '$300,000 revamp starts on Jimmy's Pies store', *The Southland Times*, 9 April 2008

Websites

www.ajpark.com/newsletters/brandscape/BRANDSCAPE_AUG_05.htm

www.allblacks.com

http://americanhistory.si.edu/archives/d8553.htm

www.anathoth.co.nz

www.bakeinfo.co.nz

www.belltea.co.nz

www.businesshistory.auckland.ac.nz

www.ceac.co.nz

www.electrolux.com

www.foursquare.co.nz

www.gsk.com

www.hubbards.co.nz

www.lpcafe.co.nz

www.lwr.co.nz

www.mlahanas.de/Greeks/Bios/MiloCroton.html

www.morgan.co.nz

www.nestle.com
www.norsewood.co.nz
www.nzedge.com/heroes/nathan.html
www.nzicecream.org.nz/industryfacts.htm
www.paeroa.co.nz
www.practicalfishkeeping.co.uk
www.resene.co.nz
www.skellerup.co.nz
www.southernheritage.org.nz/northerncemetery
www.speights.co.nz
www.steinlager.com
www.temukahomeware.co.nz
www.tiptop.co.nz
www.tui.co.nz
www.unilever.co.nz
www.vegemite.com.au
www.yarrows.co.nz

Image credits

Alexander Turnbull Library: 13 (with thanks to Fonterra Brands Tip Top Ltd), 25, 47 (New Zealand Free Lance Collection), 58 (The Dominion Post Collection), 95, 120 (with thanks to Tourism New Zealand), 131 (with thanks to Foodstuffs), 142 (Gordon Burt Collection), 154

Nicola McCloy: 22, 33, 76, 106, 163

Sheryl Forde: 50, 111, 139

Barker's Fine Foods: 72

Vicki O'Connell: 87

DB Breweries: 117

Smith & Caughey's: 133

Acknowledgements

A huge thanks to the brains trust who suggested lots of the companies and products included in this book – they are Melanie Stevens, Tree La Rooy, Kim Buchanan, Nicky Farquhar, Angela Dall-Hjorring, Angela Locking, Rochelle Preddy, Catherine McCloy, Adrian McCloy, Cathy Hegarty, Katy Yiakmis and Claire Radford.

I owe pies and beers to Leonie Freeman, Nick Turzynski, Susan Brierley, Rebecca Simpson and Jenny Hellen for their work on this book.

Deep South Hokey Pokey Bombs all round for Michelle Grace, Vicki O'Connell, Margaret Farmer, Bridget Squires and Beris Forde – I'll put the money towards the farm!

Also by Nicola McCloy

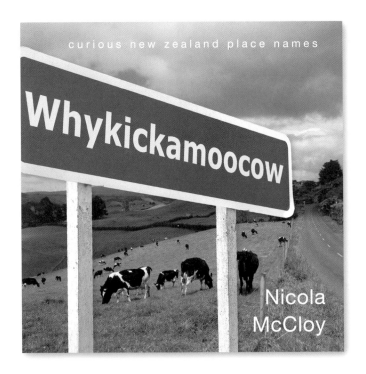

curious new zealand place names

Whykickamoocow

Nicola McCloy

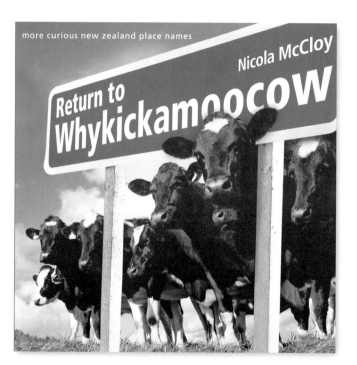

more curious new zealand place names

Nicola McCloy

Return to Whykickamoocow